T0208790

DARK JUSTICE / WHITE-COLLAR CRIMES

DARK JUSTICE / WHITE-COLLAR CRIMES

VINCENT DIORIO

ARCHWAY
PUBLISHING

Copyright © 2023 Vincent Diorio.

All rights reserved. No part of this book may be used or reproduced by any means, graphic, electronic, or mechanical, including photocopying, recording, taping or by any information storage retrieval system without the written permission of the author except in the case of brief quotations embodied in critical articles and reviews.

This book is a work of non-fiction. Unless otherwise noted, the author and the publisher make no explicit guarantees as to the accuracy of the information contained in this book and in some cases, names of people and places have been altered to protect their privacy.

Archway Publishing books may be ordered through booksellers or by contacting:

Archway Publishing
1663 Liberty Drive
Bloomington, IN 47403
www.archwaypublishing.com
844-669-3957

Because of the dynamic nature of the Internet, any web addresses or links contained in this book may have changed since publication and may no longer be valid. The views expressed in this work are solely those of the author and do not necessarily reflect the views of the publisher, and the publisher hereby disclaims any responsibility for them.

Any people depicted in stock imagery provided by Getty Images are models, and such images are being used for illustrative purposes only.
Certain stock imagery © Getty Images.

ISBN: 978-1-6657-3353-3 (sc)
ISBN: 978-1-6657-3352-6 (hc)
ISBN: 978-1-6657-3354-0 (e)

Library of Congress Control Number: 2022921127

Print information available on the last page.

Archway Publishing rev. date: 1/13/2023

CONTENTS

INTRODUCTION

The story I present here is a true account of a man who was trying to achieve success in this world. The story revolves around corruption in town and stage governments and medical communities, and it involves professional people who were corrupt. Some of the involved people worked at the town level. Others were doctors, lawyers, judges, and state politicians.

The man started his career with his own business and then went on to work for a town. His goal was to retire from his town job. Unfortunately, the turn of events changed the man's life forever as he endured multiple issues involving his health, legal matters, family problems, and financial issues.

The story started with a boss who was a superintendent at the time. This superintendent was a bully on the job to everybody. He was guilty of verbal abuse, racial discrimination, and many other indiscretions that can be proven. The abuse from this point forward was also carried out by medical doctors, attorneys, the legal system, and politicians. This new version of torture from a mental level is very hard to explain. Plus, the side effects of any mental stress condition causes physical issues that can stop anyone from leading a normal everyday life.

The federal and state laws in our country are supposed to control the criminal action of white-collar crimes committed by professional people and legal authorities, but nobody wanted to hear the truth about these problems or issues when the man complained about them through legal channels. White-collar crimes don't carry any weight in the eyes of the law until a serious problem occurs. In a one-on-one situation, a person who has a complaint has no chance of fighting the medical and legal systems of this country. That is because of the low standards of today's laws.

This story exposes the truth, the corruption, and the criminals (medical and legal professionals and legal authorities) involved with these problems and issues of *Dark Justice and White-Collar Crimes.*

The story is true; all names of places and people have been changed for copyright and legal reasons.

CHAPTER 1

STARTING A BUSINESS IN 1980

In 1980, I was a sophomore at Yellow Hills Regional High School. I was an honor student in all my classes, especially in carpentry shop. I had started my work career with a paper route when I was fourteen years old. As time went on, I also picked up little jobs—carpentry, lawn care, yard cleaning, and other odd jobs. This gave me a good start learning the importance of good business ethics. And in my carpentry business, I also learned planning, accounting, and office work.

I eventually received bigger jobs that required me to be more responsible to myself, my customers, and my workers. I worked hard and had many satisfied customers. I graduated from Yellow Hills Regional High School in 1982. My father helped me out by providing me with information on running a business; he worked with me as well.

My father told me to start by buying an updated building codebook from the statehouse library. Then he said that I needed licenses, insurance, and other necessities for my business. I also needed money. I had saved money over time to invest in my business. I named my business Vincent D'Angelo Jr. Construction.

Vincent D'Angelo Sr. was my father, and Maria D'Angelo was my mother. My parents brought me up in this world, and they taught me right from wrong and instilled in me many other important values. In a Sicilian family, the old-fashioned values are respect, loyalty, pride in who you are, and honesty—just like a good Boy Scout. Some of the various fundamental values I still cherish are common sense, education, and being all that we can be by being smart and learning.

Over time, I learned about many things from school, life, and business. I was like a sponge, absorbing all I could. I was the oldest of four children. After me came Joseph, Sarah Maria, and Anthony. We were a close, loving family, looking out for each other as we grew up together; we remained that way throughout our lives.

After I had been in business for two years after having graduated from school, it was time to expand my construction and carpentry business. I obtained a builder's license, insurance, a new truck with a plow, and toolboxes with many different types of tools. I found an accountant for my business, set up bank accounts, and took care of many other details. It took some time to put together everything before my business was 100 percent legal, but following the law was important to me.

As time continued, the jobs got bigger, and I needed bigger crews to complete them. Over time, I experienced both excellent times and bad times in business. There were bad times when there was no work because of economic problems; there were good times when I had too much work. I learned the lesson of inconsistency in business the hard way because nobody can predict the future economy.

When the economic problems started, I had to let go of good workers. When times got better, I tried to rehire them. Sometimes they would reply that they had already found other jobs. These lessons were ones that my father hadn't been able to predict for me or my business. He had only advised me that I would learn as I went along, and that applied to life as well as business.

Life lessons got more complicated and intense, and the same happened with business issues. For example, there were workers who did not show up to work, customers who tried to not pay their invoices in full, new laws that raised the cost of doing business, and the politics of business that took things in another direction. I learned over time that the government has control over everything that we do with our lives and businesses. It's impressive that we don't notice governmental policies and laws when we are children, but they impact us when we reach adulthood.

In time, I received a commercial driving license and a hoisting license. These licenses opened up newer and bigger jobs for my company and me. The idea was to cross-train with all different aspects of construction. The more I improved myself, the higher the price of doing business went. It seemed that the working person was always behind the eight ball. My father always advised me to keep trying and to never give up or give in to problems no matter how big or small. He told me to keep fighting.

I eventually bought a new truck with a plow so I could work through the winter months. In October 2002, I lined up residential contracts and subcontract snowplowing with the town of Butland in the DPW office. I also filled out a job application for full-time employment with that office. But the application was not immediately addressed because many other applications had been submitted before I submitted mine.

I plowed the streets for the DPW office for eleven years as a subcontractor. During the same time, I worked in my construction business. When I worked the roads for the residents of Butland, I always received compliments on my work. And I received the same response from the town of Butland and Superintendent Robert

Smith, my supervisor. Everyone said that I did an excellent job plowing.

Because I did a good job plowing for Smith, he told me that I was always the first subcontractor he called after all the town workers were on the job. I would come in early during storms and stay longer than anyone else afterwards to do other clean-ups in the town. Then in October 2013, I received a phone call from the town asking if I was still interested in working permanent full-time position. I replied that I was still interested.

The DPW secretary explained that there would be an interview with Superintendent Robert Smith, Assistant Supervisor Jimmy Flynn, and Assistant Supervisor Chuck Freedman. Then there would be a physical and a drug test. I agreed with the secretary, and we set up an appointment for an interview. It was to be on October 26, 2013.

When I showed up for the interview, I exchanged greetings with Robert Smith. He asked me to sit in the other room and wait for the other bosses. I went to take a seat, and Smith said, "You took my chair. What are you trying to do, take over my job?"

I told him I didn't know he was sitting there, and he told me he *was* sitting there, and I should sit at the other end of the table.

When the meeting started, Smith introduced everyone. Then he said that we needed to conduct the meeting as a formality even though he knew that we all knew each other. I agreed with his plan.

Smith then asked all the questions. First he asked how long I had been in business. I said since 1980. Then he asked how long I had been working for the town as a subcontractor. I said about eleven years. Then he asked which high school I had attended. I said Yellow Hill Regional High, Banton, Rhode Island.

Smith then asked how my grades in school had been. And I said that I was an A and B student. He asked what year I graduated, and I said 1982. That caused Smith to observe that I had started my business in 1980 and graduated in 1982. How could that be? I was only sixteen years old.

I told them that I had been working with my father since I was eight years old, and then I went to high school. I also said that I learned at a very fast pace in my carpentry shop. My teachers could not believe how easy carpentry was for me. I was the best in my business in carpentry and construction. Smith then asked why I was coming to the town for a job.

I told him that I loved my business and the work, but running it and maintaining it came at a very high price. I worked twenty-four hours a day, seven days a week. And the costs and challenges were too high for me to continue. I was getting older and wanted to work a forty-hour week instead of all the time.

Smith asked if I was willing to give up the money I earned in my business for a job that paid a lot less.

I told him I had money. I just wanted to have a regular job with benefits and regular hours. He asked if I planned to continue to work at my business part time, but I said I wasn't. My company required too much dedication to the work itself, the customers, and the workers."

He told me that he liked the fact that I had been dedicated to my job and the people involved in my life. He said he would like to hire me if the two assistant supervisors agreed.

The two assistant supervisors then agreed with Smith's decision. They also said that I would be a great asset to the town and the job.

Smith said he would hire me if I passed a physical and a drug test. I told him that wouldn't be a problem. I knew I didn't use drugs, and I was physically fit.

All the bosses agreed, and the meeting ended. The two assistants then left the office, and Smith asked me to stay because he wanted to talk to me as a friend. He asked me to sit down so he could talk to me. I asked him what he needed.

He said he knew I had been there for some time as a subcontractor, but he needed to explain how things work around there. When I asked what he meant, he told me that I already knew most of the guys—the workers. He knew I was friends with them. Then he said that he needed a person he could trust who could report to him about the guys and what they were saying about work or anything else that he needed to know about.

I told him we had a problem because I wasn't the sort of guy who snitched on anyone. I believed in obeying my bosses, but I drew the line with this demand or request. I reminded him that I had been a boss myself, and I had never asked anyone to do what he was asking me to do. I told him he had the wrong guy. I said I was there to work and put in my time till I retired. Then I asked if this was going to stop me from being hired.

Smith said that my response wouldn't jeopardize my opportunity with his office; he had just been asking me to do him a favor.

I told him he would have to do his own dirty work, and he said okay; we didn't have a problem. He told me to report to the doctor's office the next day, and we would see if I could pass the physical and drug test."

The next day, after the physical and drug test, the doctor explained that I had passed the physical, but the results of the drug test would take a couple of days. I thanked him. A couple of days passed, and I received a call from the town explaining that I had a job. The DPW secretary asked when I could start, and I said, "The sooner, the better."

She said she wanted me to begin on Monday, November 2, 2013, and I agreed.

I passed this information on to my family members, and they were all happy for me. I had a new job with the town of Butland.

At that time, my father wasn't with us anymore. Unfortunately, he had passed away in 1998 from mesothelioma, a cancer caused by exposure to asbestos. So my father missed out on the good news about my new job. He would never know I was following his steps, as he had also worked for the state of Rhode Island.

CHAPTER 2

A NEW JOB WORKING FOR
THE TOWN—NOVEMBER 2, 2013

T HE FIRST DAY ON THE JOB WITH THE TOWN OF BUTLAND WAS A VERY
good day for me because I was starting a normal life for myself. The
day began at 7:00 in the morning and ended at 3:30 in the afternoon.
All my coworkers joked around with me by saying I'd finally made it
to the DPW office of Butland. They were pleased that I was working
for the town because they already knew that my work habits and
character would be a good match for the job.

I was assigned to the garbage trucks department. Each truck
required one driver and two laborers (trash collectors). This department
was also under the highway department. The highway foreman for this
department was Scott Craw. The guys explained the week's routine
working with the garbage trucks. On Mondays and Fridays we had
the longest routes for garbage in Butland. Tuesdays, Wednesdays, and
Thursdays were shorter days, so one of the trucks would not have to go
out after lunch on the short days, and the three men would be assigned
to another job that needed to be done in the DPW office.

Cold weather started in November, and I asked Smith why he had started me in the cold months. He said he wanted to know if I was telling the truth about working through the winter. Plus, lots of guys failed in the winter because of the cold, snow, and working around the clock. It was common for workers to plow all night and work all day at their regular assignments. I asked if we could actually work for forty-eight hours straight if we had a massive snowstorm. Smith replied yes, if not longer than that. He reminded me there would also be clean-up at the town square and other places. Smith also explained that, when a new job opened up within the department, I should sign in for that job. He said that the other workers would get mad at me because workers needed to be there a year before they were even thought of for that job, and then the experience and time would also matter.

When each day started at 7:00 in the morning, all workers attended roll call and received job assignments. The first was the garbage trucks and crews—three trucks and three men to a truck. The second was the recycling truck with two men; this was considered part of the garbage brigade. The third was the mechanic shop. The fourth was repair jobs and checking pipelines for the water and sewer departments. The fifth was the landscaping and tree cutters. The sixth was street repairs and signs repair or excavating projects. When there were any problems, Smith would rearrange the work crews so that problems could be solved when they occurred. The DPW office had an emergency overnight crew who could take care of emergencies that occurred after business hours; for example, burst pipes and fallen trees. Finally, there was snow plowing and sanding through the winter to keep the public safe.

During my second week of work, a newly hired worker started. His name was Samuel Jones, and he had grown up and attended school in Butland. Samuel and I got along and become friends. When the guys took a lunch break, we would all have a conversation, and the main topic was Smith, our superintendent. The guys explained how Smith would screw the guys over. I asked what they meant, and Moe Downing said that Mark Batch, the old highway foreman, had been denied the assistant supervisor position because Smith had stopped the promotion. All the guys took turns explaining all the problems Smith had caused over time at the DPW office. Samuel explained that he had gone to school with Smith, and he said that Smith had been a bully as a child. The one person who knew all Smith's stories about damaging the careers of DPW workers was Foreman Scott Craw.

I explained to the guys that I wasn't a pushover; I would argue the issues of any problem I had and then take it to a level of legal arbitration. Moe said that I should to be careful about what I said because the walls had many ears. I asked if he meant snitches. Moe said yes. I told him that Smith had been trying to get me to snitch on the guys. Moe asked what I had said in return. I told him I had told Smith I wouldn't that. Moe said I should be worried about that answer over time because it could come back to bite me.

Meanwhile, days passed in November while we worked collecting the trash and doing other jobs. November 2013 was a very cold month—colder than past Novembers. The garbage was still picked up no matter what kind of weather conditions prevailed. Smith was the topic of conversation around breaktime and lunchtime because he was holding up the new contract for the association union for the Butland DPW office and workers. Foreman Scott Craw was upset about this. He remembered that Smith's predecessor, Larry Smalls, would always take care of the workers before anything else. Smith, on the other hand, was there only for himself. Smith would find ways of cutting back the budget and then turn the saving into a raise for himself. That year, his raise was an 80 percent! The workers needed their small raise to support their families. The workers' raise was about 7 percent, which is quite small compared to the boss's

80 percent. These are just a few of the goings on that made all the workers upset with Superintendent Smith.

Scott also explained that I would have started with a higher hourly wage if the new contract had been in place. The new contract had a physical year date of July 1. The contract covered a three-year cycle with a specific percent raise each year. Scott said, for example, that a 7 percent raise yearly would break down as 2 percent the first year and second year and then 3 percent the third year. Unfortunately, Smith held up the contract for a long time, hurting the workers and their families financially. These are problems are similar to the problems that happen in towns and cities all over the country. Workers are at the mercy of politics and policies and people who hold public office. The leaders we put in office can't tie their shoes, never mind run an office of power in this country. In so many cases, the public pays taxes for the mistakes and criminal actions made by politicians in public office at all levels of government. All the politicians in this country should be ashamed of their policy making and their conduct with regard to treating the citizens of this country. I expect this also happens around our entire world.

The month of December was even colder than November. I talked to Samuel about our progress with the town and whether we were doing well or poorly as new workers. Samuel agreed that nobody shared any information about the new workers' quality of work. At the end of the day, we saw Smith. Samuel and I asked Smith how we were working out as new workers—good or bad. Smith replied with a derogatory answer, saying that, as long as trucks were all in by 3:30 in the afternoon, we were doing okay. We asked what he meant, but he just walked away from us, leaving us both looking at each other as we wondered what had just happened.

Shortly after that conversation, the bosses from upstairs came to roll call one morning to pass out the assignments. Foreman Scott said he wanted me to stay with him that day. I asked what we would be doing. Scott said that Smith wanted me to do some carpentry work. He asked me if I did carpentry work, and I told him I did. I asked him if he'd seen my truck that I plowed with. It was full of my tools and toolboxes. And it was equipped a ladder rack to carry the ladders I used for carpentry and construction work. Scott said that the rack could have come with the truck when I bought it. I told him I had ordered the truck that way and I had gone to Yellow Hill Regional High in Banton. It was there I learned carpentry. All this information was on my application when I got hired for the town of Butland. I had been in business since 1980. I said, "Didn't Smith tell you? Have you seen my application?" Scott replied that Smith hadn't said anything about me being a carpenter or a contractor. Scott said that Smith just wanted me to do the work of a carpenter that day. I said I could do that work and much more, including the work required for all construction phases.

Scott showed me the carpentry work that had to be done. He explained that the windows in the back of the building were new and needed to be trimmed on the inside and outside. But for now, because it was winter, I was to do only the inside trim. I asked if they had a nail gun I could use, and Scott said no. I told him I had one, and I asked him if I could use it for the work. He said I could because using it would get the work done faster.

There was a total of eleven windows to trim out on the inside. I got the work done within four workdays. On the last day, when I was cleaning up, Smith asked how I was doing. I said I was doing okay, and the window trim was finished. He asked why it had taken me so long to do the work. I was baffled by the question. I told him I had used my own nail gun, which had made things easier and faster. Smith said he had heard that I didn't know carpentry." Once again, I was baffled; I didn't understand why he had said that. I asked him what he was talking about, and I reminded him about my application. I told him I'd been in business since 1980. He asked how he could know I was telling the truth. I told him that, if he needed proof, he could have asked for references when I was interviewed. As Smith turned away, he said, "You are walking on thin ice, Vince." Meanwhile, the guys complimented me on my carpentry. Finally, I saw Scott and explained what had just happened with Smith. Scott said, "Smith is starting with *you* now?"

One day during the week before Christmas, I gave a Dunkin' Donuts gift card and a Christmas card to Robert Smith to thank him for hiring me as an employee and helping me over the years when I had been plowing for the town of Butland. He thanked me for the cards and asked how I was adjusting to the job. I said fine, and I mentioned that it seemed colder that year than other years. Smith said we were going to have a bad winter. I then wished him and his family happy holidays, and I proceeded to leave the office. Smith wished me and my family happy holidays, and I thanked him.

CHAPTER 3

IT'S THE NEW YEAR—2014

The holidays were over, and it was January. Rhode Island was starting to get hit with snowstorms. There were six snowstorms between January and February. During the first storm, I was assigned an old utility truck that would be my truck for all the snowstorms that year. At the beginning of the storm, all the workers were called in to plow and sand. I picked up the keys to my truck and headed out to start it up and clear off the snow. Foreman James Great from the repair shop explained that the truck was old and served as the fuel truck for the equipment. He told me to be careful because the shift sometimes stuck. Moe told me the shift cable needed to be replaced. He said I should get as much use out of the old cable as possible; then he would replace it when it finally broke. Jokingly, I said, "Okay, Moe! We'll will drive till it breaks!"

I worked all day collecting garbage and then worked all night plowing. Then I was back to work the next day after the storm till 3:30. All the guys called snow plowing blood money. Working around the clock can take a toll on people. That is why the motor vehicle registry has laws against working and driving all day and night without sleep or rest. But our government, especially in cities and towns, overlooks these rules when snow plowing is required; supervisors allow employees to break the laws by driving too many hours without rest. This is one of the reasons commercial driving licenses for trucks are important.

For sanding the roads, we would often get a call as the night got colder or early in the morning before the public needed to be on the icy roads to go to work. Six times, DPW sanders were called in when we had snowstorms. The department used their sanders during the day when the snow melted or at night when the temperature dropped or for other safety reasons. There were eight main drivers and four alternate drivers. At the beginning of the season, the main eight drivers took all the overtime for themselves. As the season progressed, the main drivers had a chance to let an alternate driver fill in on a sanding job at night or in the morning. Sometimes the DPW office had only four drivers for sanding. On two mornings when I was plowing, there were only four drivers for sanding. The four drivers had to cover the entire town before the citizens took to the roads. One morning I was called in to work at 6:30, but my sanding routes weren't completed. When I got back to the office, I asked why I had been called back, and Smith told me I was going to work on the garbage trucks. He said he'd send another worker to finish the streets. I told him he had twelve sanding drivers, and eight of them hadn't shown up when he had called them. I told him they wouldn't be in that day either. I asked why he had called me in when he had no sanding drivers. Throwing trash onto a truck is a laborer's job, and I was qualified to do the sanding job. He reminded me that I was a truck driver and a labor. I agreed, but I told him that, because he had no other drivers, he shouldn't take me off a sanding job to do a labor job. Lots of workers could fill the labor job. Smith said he heard me, but he still needed me on the trash crew. As I walked away, I was thinking to myself that Smith didn't know how to run his work crews.

When I got to my garbage truck, I asked Moe Downing why Smith would call me in from sanding when the streets were not finished. Moe explained that Smith exhibited favoritism with some of the workers who were his "little pets." I told Moe that Smith had initially wanted me to squeal on the workers with any information he might find useful. Moe asked me how I had responded to that. I explained that I had refused because I had been the boss of my own company and would never have done anything like that to my workers. Moe got upset about what I had said about Smith's request. He suggested I tell Scott, the highway foreman, about Smith setting workers against each other. I took his advice. When I explained the facts of the conversation between Smith and me to Scott, he got upset because I was not the first person that Smith had approached with this scheme. Scott explained all the dirty deeds done within the office of the DPW, and especially those done by Robert Smith. The other workers also got upset with the situation because this was not the first time these problems had surfaced.

At the same time, Smith's "little pets" heard about the information I had shared with Moe and Scott. Scott said the current issues were the reason Smith stopped a union from coming in helping the workers. Smith had a lot of influence, and he used threat tactics within our office. Smith degraded the workers in front of the other workers, and he threatened their jobs. He used many different ways of intimidating the workers. Basically, he had free reign over the DPW office, and for him, there were no consequences.

During the second snowstorm, all the workers worked around the clock again. This time, the storm occurred on a weekend. This was helpful for the workers because they would be able to rest before Monday, a workday. Smith drove around during this storm and start degrading the plowing job workers were doing. He did this over the CB radios so everyone could hear. The workers all knew each other's routes. Smith started with my route and degraded my work plowing. I saw him on water street, and Smith saw me coming out of water street with my plow down. He began yelling that Water Street hadn't been plowed, and he demanded that someone had to get over there and clean the street. I picked up my CB radio and said, "Robert, I'm here, and you just saw me plowing. What are you doing? Robert, don't degrade me in front of the workers by saying I'm a bad worker and not doing my job plowing!" Smith would not answer the CB radio.

Some of the workers called me on my cell phone to congratulate me for standing up for myself with Smith; no one had ever done that before. Later, other workers took me aside and said I had done the right thing by standing up for myself. I told my fellow workers that I always speak up for my rights and the people I work with when bosses lie and hide the truth about problems. Scott told me, "You are the kind of boss we need for this office." He told me I was aware of the laws and workers' rights on the job and under other circumstances. I told Scott that supervisors should take care of their workers because the workers make them shine. In return, supervisors should make the workers feel good about their work, and they would shine.

Scott saw me later and explained that Smith wanted to hurt me; the signs were there. Scott said Smith had done this to other people, and there was no recourse. Smith's words were gold to the authorities in the town hall, plus Smith had grown up and lived in Butland his entire life. Even if I was right, Smith would make it wrong for me. I told Scott that I had never conducted business or treated workers the way Smith did. Scott said that Smith was a bully and a liar, a problem waiting to happen. He advised me not to challenge him in any way, including when I was right and he was wrong, especially in front of the other men. I told Scott I had good business values and that personal values are wrong in business.

I have never believed in going along with wrong people, but when I am right, I won't stop either. My tolerance goes from zero to a hundred in seconds, for good or bad. Scott explained that I would lose my job if I were to get physical. I told him I knew that problem, but I wouldn't back down either; I believe I'm a defender, not a fighter, especially with bullies. I hate bullies who take advantage of people and hurt them any way they can. Scott told me to be careful about standing up for myself with Smith and his little snitches. He told me that everything I said was getting back to Smith, and Smith would use it against me in time.

Smith backed off from any confrontation for the time being. The sixth storm came through Rhode Island; it was going to drop about twelve inches of snow. My night of plowing was going pretty well until the shift cable broke. I called James Great and explained that the cable had broken. Moe called Smith with the news. Meanwhile, Moe came out to my location and towed the truck back to the DPW office. When I got back to the office, Smith said, "You broke my truck." I started to laugh and told him he had known the cable was about to break. It was just a matter of time before it finally broke. Smith told me my shift was over because he had no other trucks to drive. I told him I could drive my own truck, but he said I couldn't because the department's insurance policy wouldn't cover my truck. One of the workers came in told Smith that he had to go home because of a family emergency. I saw an opening to drive his truck for the rest of the storm. I ask Smith if I could use that truck. At the time, we were in the office with other office people. Smith asked if I knew how to drive a bigger truck with a clutch. I looked at Smith in disbelief. He knew my experience, and he knew I had a class A commercial driver's license. In my business I had often rented trucks and heavy equipment that required a commercial driver's license.

When Smith asked me if I knew how to drive the "big" truck, I lost it! I was so mad and so embarrassed. I reminded him that he had hired me because I met the requirements of the job, one of which was a commercial driver's trucking license and heavy equipment license. He had read my resume and application. When he hired me, he had praised my potential for the job and told me that I would be a good asset. But he was knowingly trying to make me look incompetent on the job. And he was doing it in front of the workers. I finished by saying, "That is a poor excuse for you being a superintendent."

Smith said, "If you know how to drive a double-stick standard truck, be my guest and go." I told him I'd started driving a double-stick truck back in the 80s. I left the office, jumped into the truck, started it up, and plowed my route. I had no problems with that kind of truck or transmission. I heard later that, when I left the office, Smith had started shooting off his mouth. I had pissed him off with my little speech. No one had ever stood up to Smith. He was just a bully, and that was reinforced when people witnessed the confrontation between Smith and me. I had turned the table on Smith. He had tried to embarrass me, but I had turned it all back to him by telling him the truth.

CHAPTER 4

SPRINGTIME—MARCH AND APRIL

WINTER WAS OVER, AND SPRING WAS ON ITS WAY. THE DPW OFFICE staff and workers began to clean up after winter in preparation for the warmer months. Smith called me up to his office. Before I went upstairs, one of the guys jokingly said, "Look out for the Vaseline! Smith likes that Vaseline." The crude meaning was that Smith would screw you over—cover something in Vaseline and stick it up your ass, especially when he was being a prick. I went upstairs to Smith's office and knocked on the door. I asked him how he was doing, and he asked me the same. We both said fine. I asked what I could do for him. He asked if I had a heavy equipment license. I told him I did, and he asked me which one. I told him I had a 2A heavy equipment license. He asked if I could run an excavator and all the machines under that classification. I said I could. He asked if I had worked for excavating companies. When I said I had, he asked how they had conducted test with the applicants. I explained that the interviewer would take the interviewee to a site where there were no buildings. The interviewer would tell the applicant to get in the machine and start it. Then he would ask the applicant to execute some specific actions with the machine. Smith asked how the interviewer would know that the applicants could actually work the machines they had listed on their resumes. I said that was the reason for the test, which was given to all applicants for various machines and trucks. Applicants had to accomplish simple movements in the open area and then more difficult ones between trees As a boss with my own company, I made sure applicants could back up, uncouple the fifth wheel, shift the transmission, and follow road rules. Then I made sure applicants knew how to use the saws, nail guns, and other tools they would need to use.

Finally, I asked Smith why he was asking me those questions. He said he knew I had been a boss at one time, and he wanted to see how I handled testing the workers. He said a new position had opened up, and the current workers did not have enough skills to operate the heavy equipment. Only a handful had experience shifting the machines and trucks. One of the guys had recently flipped a machine over while digging a hole. Another guy had turned a machine over while loading the salt for the sanders. He said those workers didn't have any experience whereas I, on the other hand, had done excavating work and other heavy-equipment work. He said he'd like to give me the position, but I hadn't been at that job for a year. He finished by saying, "Okay, Vince, that's all I need to ask about. Thank you."

As I walked away to go back to work, I started to think about why Smith didn't have the knowledge he needed to evaluate the workers' experience. Once again, I realized that Smith didn't have the knowledge or experience he needed for his position as a superintendent running the DPW office.

A few days later, Smith saw me when I was washing my hands after I came in from the garbage route for lunch. He complained that I had not come in when I was called for sanding. I was baffled. I asked why he was addressing this issue at the end of March when the winter season was over. I said that he should have expressed his complaints when it happened, not months later. He asked why I hadn't come in when I was called. I told him I had come in two times, and then I said I also had never been not shown how all the trucks operated in the dark and with the sander. I reminded him that all the trucks were different, plus sanding in the dark makes the task more complicated. I also didn't know all the routes and streets. Smith said I was lying; I just hadn't wanted to come in. I said that was just not true. I said he didn't train the workers on the vehicles or the assignments. The workers didn't know the vehicles or machinery, and that lack of skill caused accidents. He walked away, pissed off again because he knew I was right, and he knew I had been a good boss at one time.

At this point, I started to think about what Smith was trying to do to me. I then remembered that Scott and the guys had explained to me that Smith was a bully. I had a hard time thinking negatively about Smith, but I also had a hard time believing what was happening between Smith and me. This was a difficult issue because Smith had helped me when I was a subcontractor and an employee. When he hired me, he had explained that the skills I would bring to the job would be good for the town. Another difficult issue was that, on the one hand, Smith would help people, and on the other hand, he would knock them down. My mind started going in different directions. What should I do about this problem between Smith and me? I had waited eleven years for that job with the town. The job meant so much to me, but Smith's "games" were a threat to my job and career. Smith could destroy my chance to continue working for the town and jeopardize all the time I had put into the job. I would need my job for a better future. I wanted to get married and buy a house. I wanted a new truck!

In the spring, the DPW office was responsible for repair work and new projects in the town. During the winter, I had trimmed the new windows inside the building. Scott had told me I would do the outside trim for the windows in the spring. We would do it on a Saturday and earn some overtime. I asked Scott how long a Saturday workday would be, but he never replied. So, one Saturday, we showed up for work. Scott told me to get the tools and start working. He had bought some new PVC boards we would use instead of pine trim boards. The job would take about two Saturdays to complete. On the second Saturday, Smith came in at the end of the day and checked out the work. He greeted Scott, Ben Jokes, who was also working on the project, and me. Then he started talking to Scott about the new contract and how the workers were upset with him because he had not yet signed it. Scott explained that the workers didn't have a union to help them with negotiations. There were no union rules and laws and there wasn't a proper person to represent the workers. The workers knew that Smith was in charge as superintendent, and he influenced the association union, which meant that the workers had no input when it came to problems and complaints. Because of this, why should the workers care about their work or the DPW office? The workers needed a true union to represent them and help with contracts, wages, and benefits without Smith's influence. All the workers knew that Smith had stopped the true union from entering the Butland DPW office. When workers know the truth about a boss doing the wrong thing for the workers, the workers will develop a negative attitude about the boss or anyone else who causes problems for the workers. The respect will be lost between boss and workers, and that can cause more significant problems.

Scott gave excellent advice to Smith, but nothing good came from the talk. Soon after that conversation, Smith made discriminatory remarks about Todd Williams, one of the black workers. He suggested that Todd used his color to make headway within the DPW office. I asked Smith if he was sure that was the truth about Todd. I told him that Todd had never acted that way with me or anyone I knew of. Todd was a good guy to fellow workers. Smith got upset again with me and asked me what I knew about Todd being a good guy. Smith didn't like the fact I was standing up for Todd and his rights as a human being. Nobody needs to hear racist comments, especially from a superintendent.

Things changed between Smith and me. Smith plotted revenge against me. He knew that I knew that he, as a superintendent, was discriminating against one of his own workers. Scott just shook his head and was quiet about the whole conversation. Scott couldn't believe that Smith had discriminated against Todd in front of Scott, Ben, and me right after Scott had talked to Smith in an effort to help him in his job. Finally, Smith had taken a stand; he would do something negative with me or my job.

Smith boasted about all the men he had hurt on the job and how he had cut the DPW office budget. Then, when the men did not give in to Smith and his corrupt ways, he would fire them, or he would give them such a hard time that they would quit and give up their careers with the town. When it came to the budget, Smith would cut back. With no union helping the workers, he was also able to exert personal input with the association union. This resulted in dire situations for the workers. The association union was made up of employees who worked at the DPW office. They were elected as union office leaders. There were five positions: president, vice president, treasurer, secretary, and record keeper.

Smith swayed the association union leaders and the workers because he was a bully. His role of superintendent made his bullying even easier. When the association union and the workers did not follow Smith's directions, they would have to deal with his evil ways of acting as superintendent. The consequences included loss of their jobs and other types of punishments. Smith had the DPW office under his control, and there was no one to question his authority or actions. This went on for many years until the new contract came into play on July 1, 2013.

New contracts always began at the beginning of the year, and they were three-year contracts that stipulated that the workers would receive a percentage of the current pay from the year before. The workers were upset with Smith because they did not get a raise or a new contract for July 2013. They were underpaid for their work. The workers in the surrounding towns were represented by proper unions, and they were being paid about $10 more per hour. There was no appropriate union that was independent of the DPW office. Smith was able to influence and sway the association union. Workers argued with Smith and town leaders about their lack of wages and benefits and the new contract for 2013. One of the conditions of the old contract was that the DPW workers could not strike in the town of Butland. The workers had to work at all times with or without a new contract.

At the beginning of April, Smith caught me in passing and told me I was "pushing" the problems. Another time he told me my job was on the line. Smith just harassed me—and anyone else—as he pleased. I was working the garbage trucks throwing trash all day, and all the workers knew that Smith had it in for me. They knew he was giving me a hard time.

Scott asked people to work Saturdays so we could paint the room where the new windows had been installed. This wall was about three hundred feet long and fifteen feet high. It would take about six guys two Saturdays to finish the painting. Smith saw me about a week later and said he'd heard that I had been complaining about working on Saturdays. I said I didn't know what he was talking about. Why would I complain about working when I was getting overtime? He said I had disappeared for a while during the workdays as well. Once again, I told him I didn't know what he was talking about. Then I told him that everyone had figured out that he was riding me and giving me a hard time. I told him that I was doing my job, and that was it. I asked him where he was getting this information. I told him it was either wrong information, or he was just making up lies on his own. "Which one is it, incorrect information or lies, Robert?" I asked. Smith just walked away like he always did.

When bullies are challenged, they don't know how to handle the situation. They don't know what to do when their actions are reversed back to them. Smith walked away because he knew that I was right all the time. Plus, I had been a boss myself at one time, and the knowledge I had learned from that position was a threat to him and his job. And, I knew about the discriminating words he had spoken in front of foremen Scott, Ben, and me.

CHAPTER 5

MAY AND JUNE AND THE
COLLEGE STUDENT PROGRAM

When the month of May came around, the complete workforce of the DPW office was in full swing doing projects outside. We were repairing trucks; pulling maintenance on equipment; repairing the shop, the yard, and town parking lots; painting the fire hydrants; and cleaning Butland's streets. Plus, that year, we were doing a unique project for the town square.

Smith had asked Scott to build a box for the old railroad tracks to displayed in the town square. Smith told Scott to have me help to build the box and install it in the town square. One day, a group of workers went to the town square to dig the hole that was required for the installation of the box. Scott told me to excavate the hole with the excavator. Then the guys would level the dirt and lay the concrete blocks that would support the box. As we were working, Smith showed up and walked around, watching the work. I was in the hole leveling the blocks with a level. Smith saw me on my knees and said, "Vince, it looks like you know what you're doing in the hole!" Then he walked away. Then, all of a sudden, Smith started yelling at Scott about the box. He said, "What are you doing, Scott? This is not what I wanted!"

Scott explained that Smith had given him verbal directions, and he had followed them. Smith said that Scott was a carpenter and should know his job. Scott told him that, if he had given more concise instructions on paper, then he would have done a different job. He said he couldn't know what was inside Smith's mind unless Smith put it on paper. Scott told Smith that he didn't know how to instruct the workers or plan the project jobs correctly. Smith told Scott he depended on Scott and the other workers and the supervisors to know their work and their job and get it done. He told Scott that was one of the reasons he'd been giving me a hard time with my work around the yard. But Scott told Smith he was just harassing me about nothing. He told Smith that Smith had been lying and spreading stories about me.

When I saw the way Smith had disrespected Scott in the town square and then said something about me during the same conversation, I knew things would worsen for me and anybody who wanted to help me with the situation. In all my work life, I had never seen a superintendent yell at a foreman in public or in front of other workers. It was unheard of and was embarrassing for everyone involved. Plus the superintendent who was doing the yelling was embarrassing himself.

Smith held a high position in the town as a superintendent. Still, he was incompetent and had little knowledge of the work or his job description as a superintendent. One reason for that was that he had moved up in the DPW office having started years before as a young man. When I saw that Smith didn't know the work, I couldn't believe that held that position; I had more experience than Smith, having been a business owner, a boss, and a worker.

At the end of May, the town summer job program for college

went into effect, and the DPW office was part of the program. The college program was a great opportunity for the students; it gave them a chance to earn money over the summer and learn about work and job experience. The college students who came to work for the DPW office were good kids. The office paired one student with a town employee and driver for the garbage trucks. The college students received minimum wage and worked from May to the end of August.

One of the students, Chris Baralucci, was the son of a friend I had gone to school with. We often talked about his dad and his family members as we threw trash all day. Smith had explained to all the DPW employees that we should look out for the college students. I worked with all the college students and developed some good friendships.

Every June, Smith would start picking on the college students. He would complain about how often they called in sick, and he complained about every any minor thing that students did wrong. When Smith complained about the college kids, there was less pressure on me because he had less time to bully me. At the same time, it wasn't fair that the college students were having problems because of Superintendent Smith.

The family of one of the college students, Mike, had made plans to go on vacation just before college started at the beginning of September. Mike didn't know if he should tell Smith about the vacation time he would need, and he asked for advice from several of the full-time employees. The workers told him that the proper thing to do would be to tell Smith so he could make other arrangements. That way the work wouldn't be interrupted during that time. Also, if Mike told Smith up front, he would be giving Smith a month and a half to make those arrangements. When Mike saw Smith the next morning at roll call, he explained that his family had made plans for a vacation at the end of August. Smith got so upset with Mike and told him he had two choices. The first choice was to stay home and work and miss the vacation. The second choice was to go on vacation. But if Mike took the second choice, Smith would immediately fire him. Mike was so upset. He had done the right thing, but he was going to lose his job because of a bully. Mike told Smith to take his job and shove it up his ass, and he quit. When Mike came into the lunchroom, he explained what had happened. Once again, all the guys said that they were sorry about superintendent Smith. But they told him not to worry and to have fun for the summer and on his vacation. Smith explained later that he'd had to make an example of the student because of all the students had been calling in sick. All the workers were upset, but they were not willing to challenge Smith and lose their jobs.

Smith returned to bullying me with a vengeance. He punished me by keeping me on the garbage trucks with the college students all summer. When the college students worked in the summer, opportunities came up for permanent workers to do other projects and have a break from the garbage trucks. Smith thought he could punish me, but when his little snitches told him that I liked working the garbage trucks, he was upset. He thought he could run me down by forcing me to work with the college students, but I was happy throwing the trash and running to the next set of trash barrels. When Smith got that information, he was even more pissed off. The age difference between the permanent workers and the college students was between twenty and forty years. And the younger people could throw the trash faster than the older people. Some of the employees were old enough to be getting ready for retirement. Many of the workers had a hard time with the summertime heat and trying to keep up with the speed of the college students. Meanwhile, I had no problem keeping up with the heat or the students. Summertime was a good time for me to accelerate my work efforts. The college students and I would run from trash barrel to trash barrel. We would be ahead of the truck because the truck driver had to move along slowly for safety reasons. The beginning of the summer was looking good, especially when I was away from Smith.

Once the college students became familiar with the routine of the garbage routes, we were able to complete our routes faster. It took longer to do the routes in the wintertime because of cold, snow, ice, and more trash because of the holidays. Summertime was more manageable because people would go on vacations, and the people would be out more in the summertime. The workers worked too fast with the college kids, and Smith complained about coming into the yard too early. The schedule for winter was 7.00 a.m. to about 2.30 p.m., and the summertime was 7.00 to 1.30 p.m., if not sooner than that. It got to the point that the garbage truck workers were finding places to hide from the office and Smith. Part of the reason we were hiding was that, when we returned to the office, there would not be any work for us to do, and the office didn't want people hanging around the office waiting until it was time to go home. The bad thing about the garbage crew hiding was that it would take time to get back to the office if we were needed for other work. Summertime was a good time for all the workers because of vacation time, July 4th, beach time, and having fun in the sun.

The month of June was a sad time for me. My great aunt—my grandmother's sister—was in a nursing home. She was a hundred and three years old. When the doctors explained to the family that her time was coming, I relayed the message to the DPW office that I would soon have to attend a funeral, and I would need time off. When Smith found out, he asked how much time I would need. I said I didn't know. My aunt had been like a second mother to me, and I didn't know how to handle the emotions. I'm not too good with people passing away, especially when they are part of our close family. Smith told me that my work was just as important as my private life. He accused me of pushing my job to second place. I told him that I was giving him ample notice that I would have to attend a funeral soon. And I explained that my aunt had been like a second mother. Smith said he needed workers who would do their jobs without excuses. I told him this wasn't about me; it was about family, obligations, and respect for the deceased. He asked when this might happen. I said, "When she does pass away, are you going to fire me or give me more problems on the job?" He said, "That's why you are on the garbage trucks forever." I told him that was fine with me because I could do my job all day and then go home without seeing him or hearing any complaints from him.

CHAPTER 6

JULY AND AUGUST: THE TOWN JOB ENDS

THE DAY CAME WHEN MY AUNT PASSED AWAY, AND I CALLED IN TO work to explain that I would need from Wednesday to Sunday off. I would be in on Monday. Smith actually asked the workers if my aunt had truly passed away. One of the workers said he knew of the family, and yes, she had passed. He even showed Smith the obituary in the newspaper. Another worker overheard Smith saying to the office secretary that he'd been hoping I'd been lying about my aunt passing away. He said he could use his lies against me and then fire me. Smith was always trying to find excuses to fire me. His insecurities and ignorance made him determined. He took great pains to chase me around, spying on me. He asked his little pets to report any information about me, good or bad.

These conditions continued all through July. By the end of the month, I could not take the hostile conditions that Smith was creating. The workers tried to explain to Smith that he should not be abusing, bullying, and harassing me. They told him I was a good worker and a good guy. Smith totally ignored their pleas.

On August 1, 2014, I started to feel sick. I had pains and cramps in my stomach. This went on for two weeks, and then, finally, I had diarrhea. August 15 was a Friday. The problem persisted all weekend long. I decided that, on Monday, I would call in sick and go to the doctor. On Monday, August 18, I called in to work and explained that I was ill with diarrhea, and I was going to the doctor's office. The secretary reminded me to get a doctor's note to prove to Smith that I was really ill. She said that Smith was looking for a reason to fire me. I said I knew and that I would get a letter from the doctor. I thanked her for looking out for me, and I told her it was nice to have good friends to help me when the boss was trying to destroy me.

My primary care doctor, Lori Iceberg, MD, decided to run some tests to see if there was a physical problem, but the tests revealed that there was nothing wrong. She looked at my medical records and told me I was suffering from irritable bowel syndrome (IBS). When she asked me if I had been experiencing stressful conditions, I told her that my superintendent had been giving me a hard time and threatening to fire me. She said she would give me a letter excusing me from work for a week. She also wanted to see me before I returned to work.

I dropped my letter off at the DPW office. One week later, I saw Dr. Iceberg again. She ran some more tests to see if my condition had changed. The tests still indicated that there were no diseases present. Dr. Iceberg said she wanted me to see a psychiatrist. A psychiatrist might be able to help me with my stress problems. She gave me another letter to excuse me from work for another week. There hadn't been any problems when I passed in the first letter to the DPW office. I passed the second letter to secretary Wendy Potts, who was acting boss for the day. I explained my symptoms to her: I had begun to feel sicker. I had pains in my chest, my head was spinning, I was having a hard time breathing, I was feeling weak, and I was shaking. Wendy told me to go home and take care of myself.

When I got home, my IBS symptoms increased alarmingly. Diarrhea drains people of all energy. Eventually, I start bleeding. I also began to think about what would happen when I talked to Wendy, and I concluded that I had been having an anxiety attack when I was explaining my health conditions to Wendy.

The next day I called Dr. Iceberg's office and left a message with her secretary. I said I believed I had experienced an anxiety attack the day before. I asked for an appointment. The doctor called me hours later and said once again that I needed to see a psychiatrist. Therapy could help me with anxiety attacks. That response left me baffled and hanging. I felt that she was pushing off her responsibilities as a doctor to another professional.

I set up an appointment with the psychiatrist, and the week after my second week off from work, I saw her. Her name was Dr. Vera Smits, and she asked me to describe the sort of problems I'd been having. First, I explained that I was having problems with IBS. Then I told her about my anxiety, which was related to stress from my boss bullying me and threatening my job. I told her that Dr. Iceberg had suggested that I was having problems caused by stress about my work conditions. Dr. Smits explained that I she could give me medication for my problems, and I would also need to seek therapy. I expressed concern that the medications could interfere with my job when I returned to work. Dr. Smits agreed, but she said it was also my job that was causing the damage to my health. Dr. Smits said she would give me a note to excuse me from work for a week. Then a new therapist would help me from that point going forward with my job. So, I made another appointment with a new therapist within the week of Dr. Smits's letter.

When I got the letter from Dr. Smits, I called my daughter, Jenny, and asked her turn it in for me to the DPW office. When Jenny got to the office, she saw Wendy and gave her the letter. While Jenny waited, Wendy called Smith to tell him that I was submitting a third doctor's note to excuse me from work. Smith yelled over the phone and told Wendy that I was dismissed from my job at the DPW office. Wendy asked Smith if he wanted the letter. Smith said he didn't need it because I would no longer be working there. My daughter couldn't believe that a superintendent would act in such a mean way over a man's illness. She knew her father's boss had caused the health issues that were being addressed by medical professionals. Smith refused to receive the excuse letter from the doctor. When Jenny left the DPW office, she was upset with Smith. She didn't even know him, but he was acting like a jerk above and beyond belief over a sick man.

When Jenny was on her way home, Smith called me on my cell phone. He started yelling at me, telling me I was an asshole for going to the doctors and using medical issues as an excuse for not working. I tried to explain—as my anxiety levels rose—that I wasn't lying about being sick. I told him that I had problems because of the way he had attacked me in so many different ways while I was working there. I told him he behaved this way because of his insecurity, incompetence, and ignorance. I told him he didn't deserve his position as a superintendent, and he didn't know how to handle the workers or jobs. I finished by saying, "You have been faking your job all this time—and your life."

Smith said, "You are dismissed from your job, Vince." But I told him he couldn't do that because my medical issues were directly related to the stress I experienced because of his malicious intention. Smith hung up the phone to end the conversation. My daughter walked in at that moment and explained what had happened in the DPW office. She advised me to file complaints against Smith and the town of Butland. They were both responsible for my illness.

Smith went around the DPW office boasting that he'd finally got me dismissed from my job. The workers wanted to say something to Smith in my support, but if they did, their own jobs would be at risk. So they didn't act against Smith or the town. To keep their jobs, the workers had to put all thoughts about the situation away and forget about it.

CHAPTER 7

FINDING AN ATTORNEY

I HAD BEEN KICKED TO THE CURB BY A MAN WHO HAD DESTROYED MY career as an DPW worker and injured me physically by causing stress-related issues, financial ruin, and a loss of everything that would have provided me with a normal life in our world.

The task now was to look for an attorney to handle my case and legal problems. The first question most of the attorneys I spoke with asked was, "What are the physical problems you are experiencing?" When I explained that a superintendent boss had stressed me out on the job by bullying me, harassing me, swearing, calling me names, and many other things, and even had discriminated against black people, the answer from the attorney was very cruel. The attorneys who supposedly handled stress-related cases like mine made unbelievable excuses for why they wouldn't take the case on themselves. Some of the attorneys asked how much money I had to spend. When some attorneys listened to my entire story, they explained that mental illness problems are not easy to prove. Even when I said that witnesses could testify about Smith's abuse, they observed that few workers would put their jobs on the line to help me. They couldn't afford to lose their jobs. The bottom line was that finding an attorney in Rhode Island was not an easy task.

I explored many sources in my search for an attorney, but I had very little luck. Finally, I applied online to find an attorney, and one attorney did answer me. Attorney Bob Keyhole called me and asked me to describe the discrimination I had witnessed. I told him it had involved race, age, and health. Keyhole explained that I should go before the board of discrimination, and I had only one year to file from the time of the incident. I would also have to pay Attorney Keyhole $3,000 for him to handle this case.

So, at the end of September, I hired Attorney Keyhole and gave him $3,000. In a week or so, he sent an email to the town authorities confirming that I had been dismissed from my job with the town of Butland. Keyhole clarified that my termination was their response to the fact that I had hired an attorney to file against Robert Smith and the town of Butland for discrimination.

I emailed Keyhole saying that I had been seeing a doctor to get a diagnosis for my health problems. During that process, I had been dismissed from my job. At that point, I believed that the town had discriminated against me because of my health problems. They had wrongfully dismissed me. I also said that, if they were smart, they should have waited until I returned to work and then dismissed me rather than dismissing me when I was out sick.

Keyhole never got back to me with regard to that email. About a month later, Keyhole received a settlement offer for $5,000. He asked me to come and discuss it with him. When I heard about the settlement, I was confused. But Keyhole was pushing me to accept the settlement offer. I asked him why I should accept. I had just paid him $3,000, so he had made money. I would gain nearly nothing by accepting. I told him he hadn't even seen the medical bills or the doctors' reports. "What are you doing for me?" I asked. "I'm seeing all types of doctors, and you are trying to settle the case? You didn't even ask for my explanation—my story and my complaints. What kind of an attorney are you? At the same time, I am dealing with all the symptoms of anxiety, IBS, and other stress-related problems."

Keyhole told me he'd get back to me with a better answer. I never did receive that follow-up phone call from Attorney Keyhole.

As time went on, I noticed I was experiencing pain throughout my body, and I couldn't figure out why I was hurting so much. I made yet another doctor's appointment. The Dr. Iceberg asked how I was feeling, and I explained the pain running throughout my body. He handed me a paper that contained a list of symptoms and asked me to read it. Then he asked how many of the symptoms I had. I told him I had all of them! He then told me that I had fibromyalgia, IBS, anxiety, and stress-related issues and problems that were all connected, and that was not good for a human body. I told him I agreed, and I said that my body seemed as if it wanted to explode from the inside. The doctor agreed sympathetically. Then he asked if I was seeing a therapist. I said was. He asked if I was taking any medicine? I said was. He said it was going to take time to heal. I agreed and said that the road would be even longer because I was dealing with an attorney who was not doing his job correctly and town representatives who were lying about my job and related legal problems. The doctor also said that I should try to reverse the fibromyalgia symptoms within three years. If it went longer, the fibromyalgia would be permanent. I would have to deal with it for the rest of my life, and the conditions would get worse as time went on.

Attorney Keyhole finally contacted me to say that the town had made the same offer again. He asked if I was willing to accept. I said no, and I asked him if he had talked to any of my doctors or received any reports from them. He just avoided my questions. I told him that I had just been at the doctor's office, and the doctor had diagnosed me with fibromyalgia and other stress-related illnesses. I asked him again if he had requested any information about my medical situation or asked to see my records.

One of the best things I decided to do during my struggles was to keep detailed records and even audio recording. I tracked all the problems from the beginning, including my appointments with Attorney Keyhole and doctors. The law states that recording people is illegal, but how could I protect myself when professional people were taking advantage of me? Robert Smith and the town of Butland had caused my mental stress and physical illness. A person like me doesn't have many choices when professional people break the laws of this country. I had two options: to follow the laws or violate them. How could I protect my well-being and health from liars and prove the truth to these professional people and people in authority? The problem is that, when professional people break the laws, should we follow their example? Or should we do the right thing and respect the law? Sometimes a good person has to "bend the laws," as the attorneys say, without breaking the laws. It's a sad day in this country when professional people and rich people can get away with violating the laws, and the less-well-off innocent people pay the price and lose everything they had in this world. I would not be protected from lies and deceivers, especially when diagnosed with mental stress and illness. Mental stress illness relates to the brain. I began to develop trust issues as professional people took advantage by altering my original complaints and refusing to look at medical and legal records.

I went back and forth between Attorney Keyhole and my primary care physician Dr. Iceberg in an attempt to get my medical records transferred to Keyhole. But I was receiving no cooperation from either one. Attorney Keyhole didn't request the records from Dr. Iceberg, and she wouldn't cooperate with attorney Keyhole or me. Dr. Iceberg refused to hand over my medical records.

I found it difficult to trust either of them, and this only increased my fibromyalgia symptoms along with my IBS, and other stress-related problems.

After a while, Keyhole and my girlfriend, Lisa Warren, went to a discrimination board hearing without any medical records. Plus, Attorney Keyhole's version of my complaints differed from my actual original complaints, which I had explained to Keyhole. The incidents of discrimination were not the basis of my original compliant. Still, Keyhole's version became the official complaint, and my original version was covered up and lost.

On the day of the discrimination hearing, Attorney Keyhole wasn't even prepared. He had only had one copy of the complaints papers, and he needed four—one for me, one for the town, one for himself, and one for the hearing judge. When I read the papers, I told him that what he had written didn't match the information about my complaints that I had explained to him in his office. He told me to be quiet and just sit there. Soon, the introductions commenced in the hearing room. My girlfriend was sitting in the back of the room. The town attorney, Gram Stoneman, started by complaining that my attorney was not prepared for the hearing. He said that Keyhole's complaint hadn't been adequately prepared for the judge. The judge didn't even address that issue and asked Attorney Keyhole about my complaints.

Attorney Keyhole cited racial, age, and health discrimination committed by Superintendent Robert Smith and the town of Butland. Then the judge asked the town attorney, Stoneman, about the town's disposition on this matter. Attorney Stoneman explained that Superintendent Smith had done nothing wrong. The town denied all allegations. Finally, the judge asked if I could explain the facts of my case and my side of the story. That's when anxiety hit me. As I tried to explain my complaints, I was trembling, my voice was broken up, and my head was spinning from dizziness. I tried to explain Smith's racial discrimination by telling the story about what Smith had said about Todd, a black man, and my friend. The judge asked how that had interfered with my health, and I told him that I was in a relationship with a woman of mixed ethnic background—African American, American Indian, and other races. Members of my family were also involved in interracial relationships. I considered any racial insults comments offensive beyond belief; racism derives from the outright ignorance of the human race.

The judge asked if the town had anything to say on this matter. Attorney Stoneman said they sympathized with me and my family matters. Smith said nothing about any racial comments. Meanwhile, Attorney Keyhole just sat there and did nothing to support my argument or the case. I felt as if I was alone representing myself without an attorney, even though he sat right beside me. The judge then asked what why I had indicated age discrimination. I told him that Smith expected the older workers to accomplish as much work in the same time as the part-time summer college students, who were in their early twenties. I knew this was a form of age discrimination. Men in their thirties and forties work hard but their output can never compare to that of twenty-year-olds who have so much more speed and energy. Smith explained that he preferred the more senior men because they had family and financial responsibilities to keep them working. Twenty-year-olds had no responsibilities and often didn't show up for work or called in sick. Smith often pitted the old against the young. The judge then asked me about my health problems. I told him that I had been feeling sick, and I had consulted with several doctors. Then, the next thing I knew, Smith had dismissed me from my job. That led me to believe that Smith didn't even acknowledge that my health problems could be related to my job.

The judge said he would take the information and investigate the allegations. He would notify the attorneys when he had made a decision. The hearing was adjourned, and my girlfriend Lisa and my attorney Keyhole left with me. I started to ask questions about what had happened. I told Keyhole that he hadn't even been prepared for the hearing, and he had changed my original complaints and problems. We had presented two separate complaints at the hearing. One complaint was written by Keyhole and another complaint was presented by me orally. And he hadn't even taken any notes on the case. I asked him if he thought I would win. I asked if there was any way to correct what had happened at the hearing. He said that, once the complaints were made, that was it for me. I asked him if that meant that I had lost my case at the hearing. He said it didn't; I could still win. When I asked what would happen next, Attorney Keyhole said it could take up to two years before we would receive an answer. I asked if we going to file complaints with the courts.

Attorney Keyhole avoided the question in front of my girlfriend Lisa. He gave excuses about the whole situation. My anxiety was running high, and I exploded at him. I told him he needed to give me a straight answer. He said no. He would not file court documents for the case. I asked why, and he just walked away, leaving me standing there with Lisa. She said I needed to find a better attorney. It was unprofessional of Keyhole to walk away and quit the case. I had no choice; I wanted this case to go to a courtroom and be adequately heard and legally justified. The problem was to find another attorney to accept the case and do the job the right way. When I got home to my family, Lisa and I explained how everything had happened and how Attorney Keyhole had just stolen my money and then run away.

CHAPTER 8

TRYING TO FIND A SECOND ATTORNEY

I NEEDED TO FIND A NEW ATTORNEY AFTER ATTORNEY KEYHOLE HAD left me high and dry at the discrimination board hearing. A new attorney would find the case challenging because the first attorney had made mistakes with the discrimination board. The task of finding a new attorney would take some time. The hearing date was in June 2015, and by December 2015, I had found a new attorney, Allen Moakley. Attorney Moakley asked for a retainer of $5,000 to be paid before the meeting date. He set up an appointment for February 8, 2016. He would interview me to learn about the case and to hear my explanation of my complaints about Robert Smith and the town of Butland, which had led to the loss of my job.

I asked Attorney Moakley about our procedures going forward in the case, and I asked him about the court procedures. He explained that we would file papers with the courts. One filing would be with the Workers' Compensation Office in Sealand, Rhode Island. The other would be in the superior court in Wedham, Rhode Island. I asked him about the discrimination board. Attorney Moakley said we would just have to wait for an answer from them. I explained to him that Attorney Keyhole had made many mistakes at the discrimination board hearing, and I asked if we could file a complaint against the case because Keyhole had presented the wrong information. Attorney Moakley said no. I wanted to know why attorney Keyhole had lied about my complaints. I asked if we could make the judge aware of these problems, but Attorney Moakley said no again. The town of Butland and Attorney Stoneman had presented a letter allegedly written by Scott Craw, the highway foreman for the town of Butland. The letter was filled with lies. Plus, it was written one year after the problems had occurred, and Scott hadn't signed the copy of the letter that was entered in the records. Attorney Moakley said there was nothing either of us could do about the problem with the discrimination records. The town of Butland and the town attorney, Stoneman, had fouled the case and gotten away with lying and not presenting the correct information to the court of law.

My health problems were only getting worse over time as I continued to fight more problems with doctors and attorneys and the town. I experienced more challenging problems of anxiety and stress than anyone could imagine. I was fighting my mind and the way my body was reacting. Dealing with people only caused more mental and physical stress issues. First, I had to deal with chest pains, confusion, panic attacks, and headaches. And these were only anxiety issues. Then, I had to deal with the physical symptoms of fibromyalgia body pains and IBS. All of this was stress related. If I was not able to change my fibromyalgia situation, it would become permanent, and any additional stress over a long period could make the symptoms worse.

When I hired Attorney Moakley, he explained that he would retrieve all the records from Attorney Keyhole so he would be updated on what had gone on so far. I said that would be fine. A week after Moakley received my records from Keyhole, I received a phone call from Keyhole. He asked me why I was leaving him and hiring a new attorney for the case. I told him for starters that he had walked away from me in Sealand, and I hadn't heard from him for about eight months. Also I told him that he had said he would not file in the courts, so what was I supposed to think or do? He asked what he could do for me at that point so we could continue our attorney-client relationship. I asked him if he was going to take the case to court, but he hesitated and did not answer. I told him I had already hired an attorney who would take the case to court. Then Attorney Keyhole begged me to keep him on the case. I told him we were all done, and I hung up the phone.

I talked to my mother and my other family members and Attorney Moakley about the phone call with Attorney Keyhole. We all agreed that something was weird with that conversation and the way Attorney Keyhole had acted. I wondered if Keyhole had been having conversions without my knowledge with the town officials, including the town attorney, and maybe more people. My family members believed I would never know the truth about that. I believed that I would someday, but I was not sure when. Attorney Moakley said it was possible that Keyhole had been having such conversations. I asked Moakley how his conversation with Attorney Keyhole had gone, and he told me it had been okay, and Keyhole had sent the requested records. I could only think that some kind of side deal was being made between the town representatives and Attorney Keyhole.

Attorney Moakley asked me to talk to my doctors to see how they would react to requests for their cooperation in a workers' compensation case and discrimination case. I explained that Attorney Keyhole hadn't even talked to the doctors or asked for my records. I did ask the doctors about Attorney Keyhole, and they didn't even know who he was. Attorney Moakley said it had been two years since the health issues started, and my health and stress problems had only deteriorated. I agreed that was true, and the doctors hadn't cooperated with me. Moakley said that might be a problem for the cases because, if the doctors didn't explain my problems to a judge, I didn't have a case. I said that there must be a way to obligate the doctors to cooperate; otherwise, we would have to use a different strategy. Attorney Moakley said we would work on these problems, but for now, I needed to convince the doctors to work with us. At first, I said okay. Attorney Moakley also said I should apply to Social Security for Supplemental Security Income (SSI) benefits. When I asked why, he told me that if Social Security provided benefits, that would prove that I had been injured on the job, and that would make it more difficult for the town and their attorneys to win their cause. Attorney Moakley come out strong with the correct answer initially, but would his efforts remain constant to the end of the case?

Attorney Moakley asked for a list of all my doctors: my primary care physician Dr. Iceberg, rheumatologist Dr. Orlando, gastroenterologist Dr. Sole, neurological Dr. Moel Hatcher, psychiatrist Dr. Jen Chow, and therapist Fay Pain. He also asked for a list of the facilities where I had been treated. We needed to provide signed releases to these people and facilities so they could release my medical records to my attorney.

Attorney Moakley also told me I needed to claim the settlement of the lawsuits on my taxes. I asked him what he was talking about; lawsuits never paid taxes. Moakley also said that, if we did get a settlement, say, for a million dollars, I would receive only half of the money in accordance with the courts and tax laws of this country. I told Moakley that was bullshit! No way was there any truth in his explanations of these issues. Meanwhile, my medical conditions started to act up and bother me with pains and other issues. I looked into what Moakley had told me and found that he had been lying about the laws and paying back with taxes and half settlements.

I started noticing how people were treating me, and I found out that people were taking advantage of me because of my mental stress problems. People knew that I was on medications and was going through all kinds of problems with them. In accordance with the laws of this country, people are prevented from taking advantage of disabled people or people with medical conditions. This taking advantage related to all the professional people (doctors and attorneys) involved with my cases. The problems only highlighted more reasons for me not to believe in the people or laws or anything good in this world.

Robert Smith had started the problems by taking advantage of a good worker who had no problems. I started with no health problems, and now I had many. When I started the job as an employee, I already had years of experience working successfully for myself.

Now, after I explained my issues to doctors and attorneys, they took advantage of me, and this only worsened things for me. My health continued to deteriorate.

I also noticed that Attorney Moakley initially provided the correct information in my case and then changed or left out words, causing more problems with the story. He seemed to be trying to confuse the cases more. When I asked him about this, I noticed that he talked in circles and didn't provide any answers to my questions. Similar problems also happened with the doctors involved. The correct information from my doctors and my medical health records never made it to my cases. This only provided more questions about what was going on with all the professional people. They couldn't even provide answers for me about my conditions, either medical or legal.

As I continued to go to my doctor appointments and therapy appointments, I tried to explain to the doctors the conditions of my body and what I was going through on a regular basis. I experienced different unbelievable pains. One type was aching pain. Another was stabbing pain, which feels like a knife or needles going through my body parts. I also got headaches. These pains and other conditions were only worsening over time because the doctors couldn't or were unwilling to explain these problems to me. The doctors did explain some of the medical conditions to me, but I feel that they never explained all the details. It was as if they were holding out on the truth.

All of my health conditions were stress related. One of the most significant issues was fibromyalgia. This condition caused the majority of my pain, and I know now that it will continue for the rest of my life. My IBS also had a significant negative impact on my quality of life. I explained to my doctors that, in just two years after the symptoms started, these issues had only gotten worse. I wondered what my future would be like with all the pain and medical problems. The doctors began to avoid any questions I asked. When I explained to the doctors that I had an attorney on the cases and that I would need their cooperation, they avoided the conversation. I received no response from them, and I received no answers. I had been left hanging by the legal professionals, and now I was being left hanging by the medical professionals.

I contacted Attorney Moakley and explained that the doctors didn't even want to help me with my stress, fibromyalgia, and IBS problems. I had visited all of them and got no helpful response from them. I told him that he should send letters to the medical professionals introducing himself and saying that he was representing me and handling my cases. Attorney Moakley told me that he would send letters to all my doctors, but I found out that he did not send any. He asked for medical records only from my primary care physician and my rheumatologist. The doctors didn't even know that Attorney Moakley had asked for my medical records.

I only found out over time about all the problems with the

professionals involved with my case. I intentionally watched over everyone who was mishandling and falsifying information, medical records, legal records, and many other aspects of my cases.

My personal thoughts were all about the problems I was experiencing. I thought about the health issues I was suffering with, all the professional people I was dealing with, the job that I had held for about twelve years and had loved, and one man—Robert Smith—who had destroyed my future in so many ways that it was difficult to understand on all levels. I thought about the doctors who had told me that my stress-related health problems stemmed from my job and the treatment I had received from Superintendent Robert Smith, who was supported by the town of Butland. I thought about my involvement with Attorney Keyhole, who had not represented me or my case properly. I thought about Attorney Moakley, who had started to play the same games. I believed the legal and medical professionals were only involving themselves for money reasons. Justice and good medical care were not their goals.

All the while, I was trying to deal with my stress, anxiety, fibromyalgia, IBS, and other conditions. I thought I would lose my mind with all that was happening in my life, and nobody cared to help me in any way.

CHAPTER 9

SCOTT CRAW AND THE LETTER

Attorney Moakley and I received an envelope full of papers from the law firm of BFY. The papers were pertinent for the discrimination case against the town of Butland. The law firm sent two copies, one for me and one for Attorney Moakley. Both of us went through the paperwork and discovered that that information was nothing but lie upon lie. Only I knew the truth. Attorney Moakley started to question the situation. He wondered if he should quit the cases at that point. I explained that I had found a lot of information about myself in the papers that was untrue, and the town employees and representatives had been the source of the information. Attorney Moakley agreed and said we should set an appointment and talk about the new problems and the town's offer to end this case.

On the day of the appointment, one of my family members and I met with Attorney Moakley. When we started to go over the papers, Attorney Moakley asked me, "What is this letter from Scott about you and your working ability?" I explained that the letter was all lies, and I didn't think Scott had written the letter. But it was the same letter the town had used at the discrimination board hearing. I told him I thought they hoped that the letter would discourage us about our chances of winning the cases. I had worked for the town for a long time, and I knew that Smith and the town officials would lie about anything to get results that were in their favor, no matter what the cost would be. I said that I had never seen physical evidence that the DPW offices and other offices in the town hall ever kept good records. For that reason, I didn't believe Scott had written the letter. I had also seen a worker get fired when he asked for verification about his hours for the week and his accumulated sick time. I also said that Smith had been suspended from his position as a superintendent because of a significant problem. Attorney Moakley said that Smith's history didn't matter; the situation we were facing was only about me. I told him it was also about Smith and the dirty tactics that he used against me as we moved forward with these cases.

I told Moakley how Smith had continually put pressure on the workers to get rid of the new union that was coming in and was only there for one month. I explained that Smith broke federal laws to stop a union from entering the DPW office. Once again, the workers were witnesses to how fast Smith preyed on the workers and anything else that got in his way. Attorney Moakley said again that I was the issue, not Smith. I then said that I believed that Smith had written the letter that had allegedly been written by Scott. The reports that I had not gone into work to sand the roads were lies to discredit me and my work habits.

Attorney Moakley asked me to explain the issue about me supposedly missing sanding dates. I told him that there were eight main drivers for sanding and there were four alternate drivers. I had gone in twice and missed four times when they called me. I also said that the DPW office didn't train employees to do their jobs. And one of the jobs they didn't train for was sanding. They didn't even specify the actual sanding routes. That year I was still learning the streets of Butland. I explained that, when Smith brought up this sanding issue, we were in the middle of March. He should have told me about his dissatisfaction with my work the day after the incident rather than months later. Attorney Moakley did not respond or give me any advice. I showed him copies of some DPW worker records, which Smith often kept on scraps of paper. It was written on a company pad of paper that I hadn't shown up when I was called, but where were the names of other workers who hadn't shown up either? There was no record of any phone call. Once again, I received no response from Attorney Moakley. He didn't offer good observations or say that I was wrong to ask my question. It was as if the question just disappeared into the air. I repeated the question, but still got no response.

I referred again to Scott's letter, and I asked, if Scott had written it, why hadn't he signed it? Attorney Moakley said he didn't know. I told him he should look into that because we might prove some of the lies and other problems in the DPW office that the town and Smith were introducing to the case. Attorney Moakley avoided this issue altogether, and I started to get upset with him. I started noticing that he wasn't representing me properly.

I was stuck with an attorney who wasn't working in my best interests. What was I going to do? I turned to my family members and asked them if they could advise me. I got some answers by talking to another attorney to see what he would do or say about my problems. He explained that I needed to document all the problems I'd had at work from start to finish. I had been doing this from the beginning. That's why I had taken family members with me on visits with doctors and attorneys. I wanted to be sure that people besides me heard what was said. This was another time when I felt like throwing in the towel. But I remembered what my dad had said to me when I was a kid: "Never give up when you are right." My dad always told me to fight hard to prove that I was right.

Whenever I discussed my cases or medical problems with

attorneys or doctors, my mind and body would go through such pain and torture. I would explain my health and legal issues and problems to professional people and then see them completely change my story around and upside down. It was incredible to experience that. It was as if they were manufacturing their own words and stories to fit their itinerary. They would just leave out the truth as I had explained it. These problems happened with all the doctors and attorneys involved with my cases, and eventually they would happen with many other professional people who invented their own versions of my complaints and problems.

The problems between Attorney Moakley and me escalated as time went on. I also was having problems with doctors who were not cooperating with the law of this country. Attorney Moakley didn't like me to look up information on the Internet or other sources. He especially didn't like me looking up other attorneys. I started looking for attorneys who handled malpractice cases involving medical and legal problems. I did this because Attorney Moakley and my doctors were just rewriting the laws of this country and doing as they pleased with my cases and health problems. They kept telling me that the information about Smith was not pertinent to my cases or my health problems. If Attorney Moakley was telling the truth about this, I wouldn't be sick, and I wouldn't be without a job.

I got tired of fighting everybody. I experienced no relief when professional people were taking advantage of me with regard to my health problems and legal problems. I needed to take back my life and take a stand with these professional people. I knew that my stress and pain might increase as I searched for outside help for my cases and, at the same time, maintained relations with the professional people I was currently dealing with.

Malpractice attorneys had a unique way of discrediting my story and explaining what had happened with doctors and attorneys. The problem is, when we follow the laws and report all the medical problems and legal problems to the proper authorities, we don't get good results, only negative results. I called multiple malpractice attorneys, but attorneys had to many excuses not to take the cases, and I didn't want to work with any of them because of their excuses.

In my experience, some malpractice attorneys don't even listen to the complete story from people before they refuse the case outright. So, I started to find out how malpractice attorneys protect their kinds of attorneys and doctors. But then, where do we go for justice in this country? Is this country just a big lie when it comes to the laws and the rights of the people? So, I planned to look for better avenues within the legal system and the government. But I would not give up just because people made things hard for me. Remember, I had lost everything that gave my life meaning—job, health, and financial security.

CHAPTER 10

DRUGS AND MENTAL STRESS HEALTH

A<small>T THE BEGINNING OF MY PROBLEMS, THE DOCTORS PASSED OUT</small> drugs like candy, especially when the doctors labeled me with mental conditions. The only problem was that I had mental *stress* problems, and nobody wanted to find an alternative treatment plan. Mental stress problems are different from other kinds of mental illnesses. My problem was caused by a person bullying, harassing, discriminating against, and threatening me as a person.

In the early 1900s, electric shock treatments were thought to help patients with mental illness, but they were only torture for the patients. Families allowed these procedures to happen without knowing the truth about what the doctors were doing as they experimented on their loved ones. The worst part about humans on this planet is that they will always repeat history in harmful ways by hurting their fellow humans. We trust professional people who practice medical, legal, and other disciplines as leaders in our world with terrible results. The best example is drugs prescribed to help people. I and many others wonder if drugs are the best solution for the patients. Opiates are one of the most dangerous medicines out there because they are so addictive. And there are other dangerous drugs that are pushed by pharmaceutical companies, doctors, and eventually by drug dealers on the street. Even the government and the court judges get in on the profit when they allow the pharmaceutical companies to sell harmful drugs to the public with deadly consequences. People have become addicted to these drugs while all the companies make huge profits. These powerful companies suffer no consequences from our United States government. Government representatives and agencies receive all types of handouts and bribes, a testament to their greed for money.

Very few drugs have helped patients without side effects. Psychological drugs are notorious for side effects that can leave people in a state of being mindless in the human body. Other side effects include sleeping all the time, suicidal thoughts, muscle issues, paranoia and schizophrenia, and many other problems. Many drugs cause side effects that have deadly consequences to the human body and mind. Unfortunately, scientists, doctors, and governmental agencies are approving these drugs without knowing their long-term effects. Even when they discover a long-term effect that hurts people, they still allow the drugs to be used. The result is that a lot of these drugs end up on the streets of America and around the world, with a deadly force of doom for all of those who use them.

The history of drugs speaks very loudly as it records injuries sustained by patients and users. When I started to see doctors, they immediately prescribed drugs. I asked what the drugs would do for me. The best answer was that the drugs would help me. When I asked them how the drugs would help, the doctors told me to just take them.

When I got new prescriptions, I would look up the drugs on the Internet and find a lot of information about how harmful some of them can be. Some of the drugs were progressive; in other words, patients started with a low dose and increased the dose within a short time. Patients cannot just stop these drugs "cold turkey." That could result in death! There used to be a commercial on the television that showed a hot frying pan on the stove. Someone would crack an egg open and drop it onto the pan and say that that was what your brain was like when it was on drugs. The idea was that the drugs were frying away your brain and your body. This scenario works the same way with prescribed drugs and street drugs, some of which are actually prescription drugs. Can drugs help people? Yes, but the side effects can be problematical, especially when they leave people vulnerable in dangerous ways. Doctors, attorneys, and other professionals find it easy to treat vulnerable people badly.

For pain, I have been prescribed a drug known as Vicodin (generic name hydrocodone and acetaminophen). I have told the doctors that the medication knocks me out for two days and leaves me feeling like shit and dopey. The muscle relaxer Flexerill (generic name cyclobenzaprine hcl) causes the same side effects. These medications are meant to treat fibromyalgia pain and some other conditions of anxiety problems and IBS cramps. The doctors have tried medications—amitriptyline, gabapentin, hydrochloride duloxetine (all generic names), and many other related medications for my symptoms of stress-related issues. The medications all confused my mind and body and made me feel shitty. These medications are nonnarcotic, but they carry a punch when I take them. Drugs affect the mind and body when they interact with the sensory neurons that send information from the eyes, ears, nose, tongue, and skin to the brain. Motor neurons carry messages away from the brain to the rest of the body. All neurons, however, relay information to each other through a complex electrochemical process, making connections that affect the way we think, learn, move, and behave. This can also lead to joint pain, muscle pain, chest pain, and many other pain problems. Fibromyalgia can affect the complete nervous system from the sensory neurons to the central nervous system. It can affect the entire body—brain, heart, all the organs within the chest area, and then muscles and joints, including the spine. Fibromyalgia compromises the central nervous system and makes everyday tasks difficult to perform.

Television commercials about how certain drugs can help patients always include disclaimer information about the side effects that could arise—symptoms like heart attacks or heart problems, stroke, seizures, dizziness, drowsiness, and even death! There is so much controversy over the safety of the drugs, we wonder if they are safe to use. We are responsible for following the laws of this country. We break the law when we take drugs that incapacitate us on any level and then operate machines or vehicles or do anything else that requires full mental attention. Drugs can compromise our ability to focus, and that can cause accidents that can hurt us and others and property. Remember, the scientists, pharmaceutical companies, and doctors are not responsible for our actions when we are under the influence of the drugs they create and prescribe. We must be our own watchdogs.

Legally, all drug information, including side effects, must be provided with all prescriptions. If someone takes a drug and doesn't heed the warning about not operating heavy equipment, for example, and he has an accident on the job, he could lose his job. Each person is responsible for to operate machinery or drive vehicles safely.

The medical, legal, and business systems do not work together when someone is hurt or affected by health problems. Instead, they all independently tell people to take their prescribed drugs and go to work, no matter the side effects. Then the patient may well be breaking the laws of this country. A person who has any illness is subject to an overall system created by our government in which all the subsidiary systems don't work together. Then the person ends up with all types of problems on all levels.

A new drug has been developed that mitigates the side effects of some long-term psychological drugs. One of the main ongoing side effects of all drugs prescribed for psychological problems is body cramps. There are also other side effects. This new drug can help stop many of these problem. But there is an additional side effect with the new drug.

People who take drugs that impair their focus have two options. They can either miss work or risk the chance of causing an accident. Of course, the latter choice is not the right one. No one's health and safety should be put at risk for any reason. But some people cannot afford to miss work, so they have a real problem. And they break the law by working under the influence. Family and financial issues develop when people have to miss work.

There is controversy around the issues of law, drugs, safety at work, and financial requirements. It is difficult to make all these areas work together for the protection of everyone.

CHAPTER 11

PRIMARY CARE DOCTOR, LORI ICEBERG, MD

I saw Dr. Iceberg about a year before the incident with the town of Butland. When I first visited her in August 2014 about my developing health conditions, I explained that I had had stomach pains for about two weeks. Dr. Iceberg asked if there had been any changes in my life. I explained that everything had been fine, but I was not thinking about work problems or the IBS problems. Dr. Iceberg sent me to Dr. Sole, a gastroenterologist who could make a meaningful diagnosis. Meanwhile, she ran some bloodwork and told me to return in a week. I told Dr. Iceberg that I needed a letter to my boss from her excusing me from work. It was new requirement for employment in today's world. If I stayed at home for a week, my superiors at work needed to know what was wrong with my health. She gave me a letter that excused me from work for a week but provided very little information about my health problems. I turned in that first letter at the DPW office on the same day I saw the doctor.

I saw the gastroenterologist within the week of being excused from work. Dr. Sole asked me to explain my problems. I told him I'd been having stomach pains for about two weeks. He asked if Dr. Iceberg had done any bloodwork, and I said yes. He then checked my records. He acknowledged that I had IBS, but my bloodwork looked good. Dr. Sole asked how the IBS symptoms had started. I told him I had been a victim of the peanut butter salmonella outbreak in 2008. He said that the IBS was causing my stomach pains, but I didn't agree because normally I had diarrhea when my IBS acted up. I had not had diarrhea for the first two weeks; that didn't happen until later when I started seeing more doctors and became more worried about my job security. He asked if I had been out of work, and I said I had been for a week. I told him about my upcoming appointment with Dr. Iceberg. Dr. Sole told me to see her and come back to see him in a month. He asked if Dr. Iceberg had noted the IBS in my records, and I said I didn't know. He told me to remind Dr. Iceberg about my IBS problems the next time I saw her.

One week passed, and I saw Dr. Iceberg. She ask how things were with my stomach. I said that I was experiencing more pain and frequently having diarrhea. I said that Dr. Sole had asked me to remind her about my IBS diagnoses, but she ignored me. She asked me how the diarrhea was, and I said that my stool was like brown water all the time, especially after I drank or ate anything. She said that my bloodwork was normal, and she didn't know what she could do for me. I reminded her that I was in a great deal of discomfort and that my symptoms had worsened over the past week. Dr. Iceberg said we should wait another week and see if the pain and diarrhea stopped. I agreed and asked her for another letter that would excuse me from work. As this was the second letter, she asked me what kind of work I did. I told her that I worked for the town of Butland with the DPW office. She asked me how long I had been working there, and I said almost a year as a full-time employee, but I had been plowing for the town since 2002. She gave me the letter and told me to make an appointment for the following week.

As I was leaving her office, I started to think about her questions about my job, especially that she wanted to know when I had started my job with the town. I didn't understand at that time why she had asked, but I would find out in time. At the office, I turned in the second letter from Dr. Iceberg excusing me from work. I gave it to secretary Wendy and asked her to pass it along to wherever it had to go. As I talked to Wendy about work and the letter, I started to feel ill. I told her I wasn't feeling good and I needed to call the doctor. She asked if I was okay, and I told her I wasn't, but I would keep in touch and update her. I left the DPW office and went home to call Dr. Iceberg.

When Dr. Iceberg called me back, I explained that, when I was turning in the letter, I had started to feel ill. She asked me to describe my symptoms. I told her I had experienced chest pains, a headache, pounding heart, confusion, and lost feeling and body pains throughout my body. She told me I had had an anxiety attack, sometimes called a panic attack. She told me to lie down and rest. She advised me to go to the hospital if I didn't feel better. And she said she would see me in a week. When I hung up after our conversation, I thought that she understood my problems and knew I had anxiety problems. My world was falling apart because of a boss, and now my health was in real jeopardy.

I saw Dr. Iceberg at the end of my second week away from the job. She asked how things were with me, and I told her that I felt worse with headaches, pounding heart, body aches, confusion, dizziness, IBS cramps and diarrhea, and other problems too. She told me that she wanted me to see a psychiatrist, Dr. Chow, and a therapist counselor, Fay Pain. I asked why I should see them, and she said they would help me deal with my mental stress and anxiety problems. So, I said, "That means I have mental stress problems!" She said I did. I was suffering from anxiety along with some other issues that needed to be addressed with a psychiatrist, specialist doctors, and therapist counselors. She said she would give me another week out of work until I saw Dr. Chow and therapist Fay Pain. I asked her for another letter to protect my job, and I asked her to include information about what was wrong with me. I waited in the waiting room for my letter to be prepared. When I read it, I saw that there was no explanation of my health issues. Right there, I started having an anxiety attack because I needed information about my health to be in the letter. The doctor's brief letters had created bigger problems with my job not just once, but three times. I had to drive home while I was experiencing the anxiety attack and then have my daughter, Jenny, take the letter in to work for me.

When Jenny got to the DPW office, she saw secretary Wendy Potts. When Jenny told Wendy she had a doctor's letter excusing her father from work, Wendy said that she needed to call Smith. When Wendy made the call, Smith went crazy over the phone, and Jenny could hear everything Smith was saying about me. My daughter couldn't believe her ears; Smith was like a madman! He screamed that he would not accept this letter or any other letters from any doctors. He said the doctors had not even explained specific health problems in the letters. Smith said that I was to be immediately dismissed from my job. If I wanted my check, I would have return my uniforms in person, and my paycheck would be given to me only.

Jenny told Wendy she would tell me everything she had learned. She left the office intimidated by Smith's words and his behavior. While Jenny was driving home, Smith called me. In a harassing and intimidating voice, he announced that I was excused from my job. I asked him what he was talking about. I told him that my daughter was turning in a doctor's letter. I told him he couldn't dismiss me from my job because I was sick. I asked him to give me the reasons for releasing me from my job. He did not answer my question. I said,

"Okay, Robert, I will see you in court. I hope you like jail because that's where you are going when I'm done with you!" And I hung up the phone.

When Jenny got home, she began to cry. I asked her what was wrong. She said that Smith had been yelling over the phone when Wendy was speaking to him, and she could hear everything he said about me. Jenny said that Smith was an evil man if he got that crazy over an excuse letter from a doctor. I told my daughter that was why I had mental stress problems. My medical issues were all caused by one man named Robert Smith. I told her that Smith treated everyone badly; he bullied the workers and the town residents. He harassed people, discriminated against multiple people in many different ways, lied constantly, and set workers against each other. I agreed with her that he was an evil man with evil powers. Jenny told me I should take him to court and fight for my rights. I said that Smith called me after she had left the office. I told her we had fought over the phone. He had started by saying he would not accept the doctor's letters and then he'd gone on to say that I was dismissed from work permanently. Then he had ignored my question when I asked why. I told Jenny how I had told Smith off and told him I would see him in court before I hung up on him. Jenny asked if I was going to contact an attorney. I said I would because I had lost my job without valid reasons or excuses.

After the incident with Jenny and Smith along with the anxiety attack I had when I was leaving the doctor's office, I decided to call Dr. Iceberg for an appointment so that I could explain what had happened with my daughter. When I called, I was given an appointment for the next day. At the appointment, Dr. Iceberg asked why I was there when she had seen me only the day before. I told her about the anxiety attack triggered by the fact that her letter didn't explain my health problems. And I told her about the second anxiety attack, which I'd had with my boss when I was on the phone with him. Dr. Iceberg asked me what I wanted her to do. I said that she could connect the dots: my job was a stressful place to work, my boss was the cause of all of my health issues, and I had a witness to the disgraceful way he had treated my daughter. Dr. Iceberg said all that had nothing to do with her as a doctor. I told her she was mandated to make notes about the abuse I had received from my boss so that there was a record that his behavior was connected to my medical issues. This was quickly becoming a legal issue, and I needed evidence. I told her she was ignoring the abuse and issues, and I asked her why. She said she hadn't seen my boss treat me or my daughter inappropriately. I told her that she didn't know about the incident with my boss, but I was telling her about it and how it affected my medical conditions. I asked her if she was going to help me with my medical and legal problems. Dr. Iceberg said that she had helped by referring me to a psychiatrist and a therapist. I asked her why she had not been cooperating with my attorney, Allen Moakley. She said that legal issues should be handled by an attorney, not a doctor. I told her that my attorney needed the proper medical information from her as my doctor. Dr. Iceberg said it wasn't her problem.

This battle with Dr. Iceberg went on for seven years, and she never cooperated with me or my attorney.

When I got home, I called Attorney Moakley and told him about Dr. Iceberg and how she had explained to me her situation with regard to my legal issues. I told him that the doctor wasn't going to cooperate with me or him, and that Dr. Iceberg felt that my legal issues were not her problem. I asked Attorney Moakley what lawful means we could use to get this doctor's cooperation using lawful means. Attorney Moakley said that I was screwed if the doctor wasn't in my corner. I would have no cases. I asked him if there were laws that could hold her responsible for her actions, but he said no. She had free will to do as she pleased with no consequences to her profession.

I ended up getting mad with Attorney Moakley. I told him he was wrong. I knew things about the laws of this country. I told him he wasn't fighting for my rights; he was taking advantage of the mental stress I was experiencing. Attorney Moakley tried to reassure me about the doctor. I told him that the town representatives had been lying, Attorney Keyhole had messed things up, and now Dr. Iceberg was not cooperating. I was losing the battle before I even got up at bat in court. "Are you nuts, Allen?" I asked him. I told him I felt as if everyone involved was taking advantage of a person with handicap problems and mental-stress health conditions. He had disregarded my complaints and the true story about the whole situation. Everyone involved was intentionally dropping the ball. The cases were falling apart while those who were against me helped themselves to personal profit. There are so many ways to discriminate and break the laws, and they all hurt me as well as other people. Some people asked why I had cracked or gone on a rampage. These are just some reasons.

CHAPTER 12

PSYCHIATRIST DR. CHOW AND THERAPIST COUNSELOR FAY PAIN

Dr. Iceberg referred me to psychiatrist Dr. Chow and therapist counselor Fay Pain to help me with my mental stress, psychosis, depression, sleep disorder, and many other issues that I experienced over time. I needed to provide the DPW office with information that I was seeing these two medical professionals, but Dr. Iceberg hadn't included the information her letters to the DPW office. Neither was she passing it along to Attorney Moakley; we were looking for this information. I now believe that Dr. Iceberg started all the problems. She refused to cooperate first, and then the other doctors and the hospital she worked with also refused.

When I went to my first appointment with Dr. Chow, she asked why I was there. I explained that my primary care doctor, Dr. Iceberg, had referred me because of mental stress and anxiety caused by conditions at my job. Dr. Chow said I was also there for treatment of psychosis, depression, sleep disorder, and other issues. I said I had not been aware of all this information; Dr. Iceberg hadn't explained all my health issues. Dr. Chow asked what had happened to me to cause me to be in her office with her that day. I explained that I had a job with the town of Butland, and my boss was bullying me, harassing me, discriminating against me, threatening my job, and doing other things to me for no reason. This had led to my physical and mental troubles. I told her that I was fifty years old and had never been released from any job. I had never had any negative associations during my entire working life. Meanwhile, I also had a family that depended on me to provide for them. I had planned to retire from my job with the town and finish my life in good condition with my family. All of this disappeared when my boss started all these problems. I told her I had about twelve years of total time working for that town department, and all the benefit it could have provided was lost. I had no work backup plan, and I had to deal with a lot of health problems.

Dr. Chow said she could see how I would feel betrayed by Robert Smith. She asked how my relationships were with the other workers. I told her we had all got along for the twelve years I had worked with them. And that was another reason I couldn't understand why Smith would do what he did to me. Dr. Chow asked how my relationships were with my family members. I told her they depended on me, and we got on as well as any other family. She said it seemed that all my problems stemmed from my job and nowhere else, and I agreed, adding that it was only my boss Smith who gave me a hard time, not any of the other workers. She said she had a hard time believing that it was only my job that had caused my health problems. When I asked her what she meant, she said we would talk about it at my next appointment in a week's time. For now, she wanted to prescribe some drugs that could help me. She asked if I was seeing a therapist, and I told her I had an appointment with Fay Pain. Dr. Chow said she knew her and asked when I would be seeing her. I told her it would be the next day, and she said she would talk to her about me. I asked

Dr. Chow how the prescription would help me, and she explained that it would calm me down so I could be at ease with myself, and it would help me sleep at night. I said that Dr. Iceberg had given me some drugs for those same issues, but they hadn't helped me. Dr. Chow advised me to take the drugs she prescribed, and at my next appointment, we would evaluate how I was doing with them.

The next day, I saw therapist Fay Pain, and we went through the usual introductions and the questions of why, how, when, whom, and the usual necessary information required for patient evaluation. I explained the same story and complaints to Fay as I had to Dr. Chow and many other doctors and attorneys. Then Fay said she had spoken to Dr. Chow, and together, they had come up with a plan. We would all come together the following week and talk together for a session. I asked if this was a standard procedure. Fay said that she and Dr. Chow needed to understand the issues and make sure they were both getting the same story from me. I told her that I had told only the truth from the beginning and that many people involved with this whole case had been screwing things up. Fay said that wasn't the problem. She and Dr. Chow had realized how excited I was, and they were worried about my health. I asked if she was being truthful or if they were afraid that I might hurt them. I said that I didn't believe in hurting people unless I was defending my life at a physical level from a fight. I had been hurt by everybody involved in my cases, and now I felt I was being hurt by Dr. Chow and therapist Fay Pain. If I were going to hurt anyone, it would be the person who had started my problems, Robert Smith. All the people involved were adding more problems by not help me and then making me feel as if I was the crazy person! The most important reason I had for not hurting anyone was that I had initiated two lawsuits; I was not going to jail for the wrong reasons.

The following week I saw Dr. Chow and Fay together. During the meeting, I discovered things nobody would believe, including me, even though I was there. The mental abuse in this country is overwhelming, and it occurs at every level of society—families, the workplace, government, etc. When the meeting started, Dr. Chow asked me if my father had abused me. I asked her what that had to do with my problems with my job and my boss. I got no answers from her. She then asked if I had been sexually abused by my father or anyone else. Once again, I asked what that had to do with my job or my boss. Once again, I got no answers.

Then Dr. Chow and Fay started to double team and ask me questions about my family. It seemed as if they were trying to break me and make me give in to their drilling tactics. This is when I said, "What the hell are you trying to do to me?" I told them that my family was not the cause of my problems and health issues; those were caused only by my job and my boss. I also said that, if they called what they were doing helping, they were both wrong. I told them they were only causing me more stress. I asked if they understood why I was there looking for help. I got no answers again.

Dr. Chow asked if I was taking the drugs she had prescribed for me. I told her I wasn't and asked her why she was trying to keep me under the influence of drugs so that I had no common sense. They kept me from thinking straight about my complaints about the town and my boss. I told her that all the doctors passed out drugs like they were candy. They are worse than the drug dealers on the streets. Dr. Chow said that, if I didn't take medicine, she couldn't see me. I said that would be fine! "I'm all done with you. You accused my family of causing me harm when the problem was my job and boss only."

The new problem that developed was that I had no trust in any professional people. What was I supposed to think when a doctor suggested that my family was involved in abuse when my complaints were against the town of Butland and Robert Smith? So on a mental level, in my mind, I wanted to hurt the people who had put me in that position, who had caused me stress and pain among other problems.

I found it difficult to control the rage inside me, but leaving the office would help me get over the feeling. I wanted to calm down and put my dealings with these people and my cases in perspective for myself and my future.

About a week later, I received a phone call from therapist Fay Pain. She asked me to make an appointment to see her. I asked her why she wanted to see me, and she said we could talk about my problems and issues. I asked her if she was going to attack me with lies and insinuations, and she said no. She wanted to help me. The joint meeting had been Dr. Chow's idea because she believed I had been hiding problems with my family. I told Fay that I had explained to Dr. Chow that my problems had been caused by work-related experiences only. I had gone to see them because my primary care physician, Dr. Iceberg, had referred me to them. I didn't understand how the information I had given all the professionals had got so screwed up. Fay said again that she would like me to go to her office. She wanted to try to help me with my problems. I agreed to make an appointment. My stress was so built up inside me that I had started to have pains running throughout my body. The headaches, joint pains, stabbing pains, neck and back pains were going up and down my spine, and my muscles were cramping up so tightly I didn't know what to do except call the Butland fire dept.

I was rushed to the hospital in Brock and was seen by the doctors there. They ran tests to determine what was wrong with me. The doctors said that I had all stress-related issues, but I also had one new problem—fibromyalgia. They told me that my stress issues would cause fibromyalgia pain that would worsen over time. The doctors said I needed to take a muscle relaxer and Vidicon for pain. I explained to the doctors that I was sensitive to many drugs. The doctors explained that the fibromyalgia could be causing that sensitivity. They suggested that I could find more information about fibromyalgia on the Center for Disease Control (CDC) website. The advised me to rest and take the prescribed drugs until I could control my stress problems. The doctors asked if I was seeing anyone for therapy. I told them about Dr. Chow and Fay Pain, and they said they would notify them of this new diagnosis. I should go to see them in a month, during which time I was to take the prescriptions.

After I was released from the hospital, I had to make a follow-up appointment with Dr. Iceberg, and I had to call therapist Fay to schedule an appointment in a month. During my appointment with Dr. Iceberg, I asked her about the diagnosis of fibromyalgia, and she said that she didn't believe in that medical condition, and other doctors also don't believe in it. I told her that fibromyalgia had been written about in medical books and on medica websites as a stress-related problem and a mental stress disorder. Dr. Iceberg avoided my questions and asked if there was anything else she could do for me. I said yes. The doctors at the hospital had told me to have a follow-up appointment with her. I said I had asked her about fibromyalgia, and she had blown me off as if I didn't exist; indeed, she had told me that she didn't even believe in this medical condition that was widely acknowledged. I said, "What kind of a doctor are you? You don't help your patients, especially when there are two legal cases involving an attorney. You don't give the proper medical records and information to the attorney or me. If I change doctors, the town attorneys will say that I'm shopping for new doctors who will go in their favor in court. Then the judges will just frown upon these issues and will rule against me." I also told her that she was contributing to the stress I was experiencing because of my job and my boss.

Dr. Iceberg said I could always change doctors if I was unhappy with her. I told her I was done with that day's visit. She said she would see me in three months, and she gave me a referral to Dr. Orlando, a rheumatologist. I asked her if I had a choice. Once again, the fury and rage that ran through my body were incredible. I had to find a way to calm myself down without getting into trouble. As I drove home,

I thought that music might calm me down. Music had always helped me throughout my life in so many ways. Music is so incredible; it can aid healing, inspire happiness, express love. It can make us feel better when we are sad. Listening to music helped me control the stress and the aggravation caused by these professional people who were intentionally throwing my health issues around. They had no cares in the world and didn't care what happened to me.

CHAPTER 13

ATTORNEY ALLEN MOAKLEY, DR. PETER ORLANDO, AND THERAPIST FAY PAIN

I CALLED ATTORNEY MOAKLEY TO REPORT ALL THE NEW INFORMATION about my health and my relationship with Dr. Iceberg. I explained that she was not a good doctor. He told me that I still needed her for the records and medical information. I told him that she was not working with us; rather, she was working against us. I said there must be a way to report Dr. Iceberg's criminal actions to authorities. I told him that she was the doctor who had primary control over my medical needs. Then I told him that the psychiatrist, Dr. Chow, had tried to insist that everything I had been going through was related to my having an abusive father and other family problems. I insisted that my family hadn't caused my stress issues. I told him that we had major problems with all the doctors who were treating me, and I needed him to contact the proper authorities to file complaints. Attorney Moakley said there was nothing he could do for me; all he could do was go forward in the court cases with the information we had.

I told him we didn't even have a chance of winning these cases because the doctors involved were not providing enough medical information and records. We were depending on doctors who were not following the laws and cooperating with us. I thought for a moment and then asked him what the chances were that the town had any influence over these doctors and even him as my attorney. He assured me that it was against the law for the town to do any dirty deeds like that. I told him that I was talking about the doctors breaking the law. I told him that I knew that people could be bribed. Attorney Moakley avoided these questions. He said he had another case to work on and told me to call him if more problems arose. The sad part of history is that doctors, lawyers, law enforcement personnel, politicians, and others have been bribed throughout history. It all comes down to money and power. Greed destroys so many people worldwide.

I asked my family to come together so that we could talk about the issues of my case. I felt I needed their advice and guidance. We started by discussing all the questions and explanations that Attorney Moakley had provided during my office visits with him. My mother said she couldn't believe what I was going through with Attorney Moakley. My brother Joseph said that the actions of the medical and legal professionals was illegal. He advised me to report them to legal authorities. If I did that, I told him, I would be rocking the boat, and the attorney could walk away. My sister, Sarah, and my brother Anthony agreed that I was between a rock and a hard place. Anthony suggested changing attorneys. I told him that I didn't have an unlimited budget. I said that the doctors had a lot to do with my problems. Without the proper medical evidence and records going to the attorney, the cases would be lost. Joseph asked me how long I had been bounced around by all these people, and I said it had been about three years. He said I should just try to get through the cases and get the best deal I could. Then I should change all the people involved, start with new professional people, or report the issues, problems, and crimes to law enforcement. My mother said that nobody can beat city hall. I got upset her and said that I didn't accept that idea. The laws are written to protect the innocent and righteous and to provide justice. I had a hard time believing that some people felt they were above the law and justice. I always try to strictly follow the laws of this country. I was determined to get justice one way or another by following the law.

I told them all that, while I had been dealing with legal issues during the past three years, my symptoms had been going out of control—anxiety, IBS, depression, psychosis, and fibromyalgia. I also anticipated a lot of other new problems that would come in time. I had trouble trusting the doctors and other professionals who could provide no accurate information about my medical conditions and who would not pass my medical information on to Attorney Moakley. In addition, he did not fight hard enough for his client or register grievances against the town and their attorneys and doctors.

I had told them all the true story, and I said that the professionals I was working with were changing the story from the original status and truth to lies; people were being deceived in so many ways. It all started with Smith and other town representatives who told their version of lies. They had been altering my case from the beginning. Then the attorneys had added their version of the lies, and they had falsified legal records. The doctors had then lied about my medical records. My mental health had been adversely affected on so many levels. It was as if my mind was going to explode with all the pressure from all these lies told by professional people.

The worse part of these problems was that nobody wanted to hold Smith and the town of Butland responsible for what had happened. An admission of fault could cause the loss of money to individuals and the town itself. And no one wanted to report criminal actions against the professional people involved. It could reflect badly on those who made the reports. So everybody remained quiet about the criminal actions, and everyone who was guilty avoided prosecution for disobeying our laws.

I had an appointment with Dr. Orlando, the rheumatologist. He would treat my arthritis and my fibromyalgia. When he asked what was wrong with me, I told him I had arthritis and fibromyalgia and that fibromyalgia was a new health condition for me. He looked at my records and told me I also had anxiety, depression, psychosis, headaches, and other problems. I agreed and told him that all my symptoms were stress related and that they had started when my boss, Robert Smith, began to bully and abuse me. Dr. Orlando avoided this explanation. I explained him that fibromyalgia was causing intense pain in my hands, feet, and spine, and I was having headaches. I was experiencing secondary pains in my muscles, jaws, and chest. My scalp hurt when I touched it or brushed my hair. Dr. Orlando said that some of these symptoms overlapped and some didn't. He said I had arthritis in my hands, feet, and other joints, and that the fibromyalgia affected all that pain. He said that the headaches and the pains in my spine were a different issue, and we would have to watch my condition and my body to find out more about them.

Then Dr. Orlando announced that he didn't believe in fibromyalgia. I told him it was written about in medical books and on trusted websites. I asked him what he thought about all my conditions being stress related. I asked if the problems worked off each other to intensify the pains. He said they did. One stress-related condition could intensify because of other stress-related condition. If that was the case, I thought, then that is how fibromyalgia is working overtime with the pain and stress. Plus, I told him that I had been fighting doctors and attorneys as well as Smith and the town of Butland because of their lies and because they had changed the complaint around against me.

Dr. Orlando said that had nothing to do with him. I said it certainly did because I was sick due to stress. And the stress was related to my former work conditions and then to my problems with the professional people involved with my cases. Dr. Orlando just avoided my statement. He said he would prescribe a drug that would help with the pain and relax me. I told him that I already had a lot of prescriptions that were meant to do the same thing. I also told him I was highly sensitive to all the medicines. I had been told that was because the fibromyalgia had affected my nervous system. Once again, he just ignored my words and said he would see me in three months. I left the office so upset with yet again another doctor.

When I went to my third appointment with therapist Fay, she asked how I was doing. I said not so good, and she asked why. I said I was fighting with everybody involved with me and my cases. Fay asked if I thought that perhaps I was the problem because I was not cooperating with people. I said no, it was because people were trying to push my buttons and then push me off the cliff's edge as if I'm the crazy one, and they're not crazy for lying about the complaints. I believed that people were intentionally trying to get me to retaliate and break the law. Their ultimate goal was to get me committed for mental issues. I saw how things worked for people in similar situations. They had no chance to win, and they ended up getting arrested for defending themselves. Nobody listened to my complaints of Smith's abuse and the stressful condition he and the town had caused. Then I had been subjected to unprofessional treatment by medical and legal professionals. Smith and the town were being protected while I had been left in the dark as if I didn't exist. These people were freely able to damage me and get away with it. Fay said that people were trying to help me, but I wasn't able to see it that way. I told her I had a real problem because Dr. Chow had suggested that my father had abused me and that my family was causing me problems.

Fay told me that I had misunderstood the reason behind those questions about my father and my family. She said that she needed to ask me some questions, and then she wanted me to fill out a computer questionnaire. She asked me if I wanted to hurt myself. I said no. She asked if I wanted to hurt anyone else. I said no. And I asked her why she was asking stupid questions. I said I had already told her that I was not a violent man. I only believed in defending myself on a physical level when my life was threatened. I told her that her questions were a perfect example of people pushing my buttons intentionally to get me to react and violate the law. Fay told me they were not trying to hurt me; rather, they were only trying to help me. I said we would see the truth in time. Fay gave me a computer so I could complete the questionnaire. There were about forty questions. Some asked if I would hurt someone or myself. In time, Fay betray me for a second time when she used the results of this questionnaire against me.

I looked for guidance from my family multiple times as I dealt with my case-related problems. I almost always took a family member with me when I visited the doctors and attorneys, but sometimes I had to be on my own. One of those times, when it was difficult for my family members to get away from their obligations, I was alone with therapist Fay. Nobody in my family could ever believe that a therapist would turn against me in any way. My family members started to see that I was right when I said that the professional people were causing problems with these case. I always told my family members how the therapist explained things to me and how she would flip things around on me. The dire situation was that I needed to see a therapist for the cases because Attorney Moakley said I didn't have a case without a therapist. The hardest thing was that nobody wanted to cooperate with any part of my problems. The legal and medical professionals intentionally damaged the cases and me. My family members tried to help me the best they could.

Still, lies, manipulation, false information, and many other ways of changing the actual outcome of cases are impossible to stop when you are going up against professional people. When I looked up the definition of discrimination, I read the following:

1. An act or instance of discriminating or of making a distinction (http://www.danboone.me/indiana-law-and-holy-week/)
2. Treatment or consideration of, or making a distinction in favor of or against, a person or thing based on the group, class, or category to which that person or thing belongs rather than on individual merit (https://quizlet.com/517885160/dwc-cultural-competencediversity-flash-cards/)
3. The power of making fine distinctions; discriminating judgment (http://www.danboone.me/indiana-law-and-holy-week/)

Laws don't explain the right way for people to behave; they only provide categories, and if a negative act doesn't fit into a category, it's not discrimination. There are many areas of the law that work the same way, and the medical and legal professions can take advantage of them. The way people fit the laws to their needs rather than for the common good of the public is incredible. The minute that people don't properly follow the laws, chaos and anarchy start to creep in and take over the people and the land. Almost all human beings want revenge when people do wrong to other people. The people who started the problems don't expect their victims to push back against them. We must have proper laws for the people in our world. But when people can change or bend the laws to fit themselves or circumstances, the laws are not working. People bending the rules is a type of discrimination. Individual merit is precisely how the laws forget that individual people discriminate against each other. Significantly, when the laws and officials discriminate directly against ordinary citizens, individuals, and groups, I always look for better answers to my legal and other problems. I never like people who lie, cheat, or steal, or commit any other crime. The seven cardinal sins of this world are:

1. Pride
2. Greed
3. Lust
4. Envy
5. Gluttony
6. Wrath
7. Sloth

Each of these can be overcome with the seven corresponding virtues:

1. Humility
2. Charity
3. Chastity
4. Gratitude
5. Temperance
6. Patience
7. Diligence

I acknowledge the seven cardinal sins of the world, but I believe that those people involved with my cases did not. The best people have the correct answers, practice patience, and are diligent in their lives. This applies well to medical and legal professionals.

In time, all people show their true colors—who is right and who is wrong, who is good and who is bad, who is a criminal and who is a good citizen who told the truth even when nobody wanted to hear it. I find it difficult to accept that official authorities can be criminals. Still, the reality of history is that men and women always commit criminal actions over their lifetimes. I know I'm no angel in this world, but I try my hardest to follow our existing laws and the proper ways of this land. I try to treat people fairly and honestly. However, when I have to defend my own life or the lives of my family members, am I doing the right thing, or am I being ignorant of the laws and the people? I will question my actions even if I am following the laws of this country and the people. The human conscience is a powerful inner feeling about ourselves that helps us make the right decisions for our lives and the lives of others. I learned how in time. I knew that I had to defend myself against Robert Smith, the town representatives, the doctors, the attorneys, and anyone else who was involved in my court cases.

CHAPTER 14

WRITING LETTERS AND
REPORTING THE CRIMES

I TOOK THE ADVICE FROM MY FAMILY AND BEGAN TO REPORT THE issues, problems, and crimes I had experienced to the proper authorities—or so I thought. I wasn't the best writer for this task, but I was the only one who could tell the true story and list my complaints correctly. My multiple health problems interfered with my writing of these letters, the major one being anxiety. As I wrote, I was forced to revisit living the abuses, harassment, and discrimination that started with Robert Smith and continued to the present time with my medical and legal professionals. The lies and deceit from all these people made my health issues and my everyday life difficult to deal with. It was as if all the lies turned me into a perpetrator in some crazy or criminal way against Smith, the town, my doctors, and my attorneys.

The facts and evidence proved that Smith and the town representatives were lying, and I was not. And the doctors and attorneys were abusing me by not upholding the laws that governed their actions with me as a client and patient. It's tough to concentrate on anything in life when anxiety attacks and other stress-related health issues impact daily life. My mind seemed to be bouncing inside my skull, and my heart often banged like a drum. I would lose my breath and gasp for air. Then I would have to deal with pain that started kicking in all over my body. Then my stomach would make me run to the bathroom with diarrhea and cramps. Fibromyalgia would then take over, making me feel as if someone was scrunching up my body like a piece of paper. I had no way of stopping the pain, and it was a killing pain beyond hell.

I had problems sleeping, sitting, standing, walking, and pretty much doing anything with my body. When people can't escape the pain, they sometimes start thinking of suicide as the only relief. I often felt that my head was about to explode because of the headaches. Then I would feel stabbing pains as if someone was pulling on my joints and trying to rip them from my body.

I didn't take any medicine to dull my pains while I wrote all my letters except for ibuprofen. The pain medicine Vicodin and the muscle relaxer Flexeril made me feel as if I wasn't in this world. I felt I was in a never-ending fog. This was partly due to my fibromyalgia and the way the nervous system works with drugs, including prescriptions, street drugs, and alcohol. Dr. Orlando explained to me that the nervous system is like a house wired with electricity, and the lights are all turned on forever with no off time. Eventually, that nervous system burns out somehow, and no one can predict how it will happen. He said that, over time, I would become a prescription user and would be hospitalized because of how badly I would be suffering from fibromyalgia.

My health had been considerably compromised in just about three and a half years, and Dr. Orlando said it would only worsen over time. I worried about what would happen as I aged.

The first letters I wrote were to the following people and agencies:

- The governor of Rhode Island
- The attorney general of Rhode Island
- The Federal Justice Department in Washington DC
- The Sealand office of the Federal Justice Department
- The district attorney of Norfolk County
- The district attorney of Suffolk County
- Two Rhode Island senators
- The four main news stations in Rhode Island

I asked them all for help, and I tried to report the criminal acts of Robert Smith, the Butland town representatives, my own attorneys, and my own doctors.

Over time, judges became involved with these cases, and their judgments had devastating consequences because they were against me. I blame the judges entirely and directly, but they can also be held responsible for trusting attorneys and doctors and not looking into any problems caused by those who did not do their jobs properly. Because of them, the judges were not provided with my medical and legal records. I consider this withholding of evidence illegal. At the least, it misled the judges and caused them to issue judgments against me. I tried to explain this to the judges, but they told me to let the attorneys handle the cases. The disregard shown to me by these judges made it difficult for me to stand up for my rights. I was being poorly treated by the attorneys who painted me as the bad guy when they were guilty of causing all the problems with my cases.

I guess that it is an unwritten law that we shouldn't report the criminals or crimes to authorities in this country. If we do, we have to deal with the destructive results of our actions. I have been painted as bad person just because I tried to stand up for my rights.

I got no results from this first set of letters even though I was trying to follow the law. This only crushed me further and made my health problems worse.

My fibromyalgia became more serious as time went on. I took time to try to heal myself when the doctors didn't want to cure me. They only wanted to give me medicines that didn't help, but the prescriptions caused side effects that made me useless as a person. Between dealing with the doctors and attorneys, I had to think about the best way to fix or heal myself. I needed to take myself to a mental level of healing and then a physical level of healing. So I began to look up as much information as I could about my health conditions and the laws of this country. I revisited everything I could remember about my two legal cases and the professional people involved with them. I was going to make sure that the public knew the truth about our government, attorneys, and doctors. There were professional people who were criminals who were hurting and isolating people like me.

I did a lot of things to help keep my mind busy and not distracted by thoughts about my medical and legal problems. I spent time listening to the music that I had grown up with. Studies show that music has healing powers. Most doctors don't even know this. Listening to music and singing along helps me emotionally. The good feelings I experienced from the music motivated me to clean the house, cut the lawn, and stay busy by following a day-to-day schedule. I needed to improve myself and fight harder, mentally and physically, especially when my attorney wasn't doing the job he was paid to do; in other words, he was only stealing my money and doing nothing for me.

I also spent some time remembering my dad and the teachings that he passed on to me when I was a child and then all through my life until he passed away. My dad always knew that I wouldn't stop until I proved people wrong if they were doing something wrong. Sometimes he would advise me to just let something go. Some things are not worth arguing about even if you are right, but my dad always knew that I wouldn't do that; I wouldn't let go. My dad knew that, for the right reason, I would fight till the end and prove that I was right.

I had a strong bond with my family members, and nobody could break that bond. The strange thing about Italians is that they can hurt each other, but no one should ever jump between them because then two Italians would fight the one who intervened!

The music I grew up with was the best music in the world. I remember from the forties to the present, but the music from the sixties to the eighties is the best to me. I share the feelings of the singers and the bands from that era. And the music helps me express so many of those feelings. Music helped me with my anxiety and helped me to concentrate on what was important to me and my cases. Listening to music also helped me write better letters as time went on. I was able to get my mind together and stabilize my thoughts, and this gave me hope that I could fight these people on their level of bullshit (lying, deceiving, misleading). I was being forced to accept their illegal answers and judgments, and I was going to challenge them. This gave me the greatest hope of all.

So I also decided to write a second letter to all of the officials and authorities that I had already written to. The second letter would be better, and I would clearly describe issues, problems, and criminal acts. I believed that the law and honest people of authority would help me win my cases.

I wrote these second letters and described all the issues—health problems and criminal matters. It took me days to write them; someone else could probably have done it in one day. I had to use a dictionary and computer to help with spelling and grammar so my letters would look professional. I put so much effort and time into these letters, and I was so relieved and proud when I sent them out as soon as they were finished. Once more, I waited for a phone call, email, or a letter, but I received no response from anyone for days, weeks, and then months.

Once more, I felt as if the authorities were protecting the doctors, attorneys, judges, and even themselves. It is amazing that the police and politicians want the public to follow the laws, but they feel that the laws don't apply to them. They get away with breaking the laws of this country. I noticed that the politicians didn't like the rush on their capital building in Washington DC. So why do they tread on the public and their hardships? The police have a neighborhood watch for crimes; maybe the public should have politicians watch for politicians' crimes. Perhaps the public should have a website for the crimes of the rich and powerful. That includes members of "high society" along with the lawmakers and law enforcers. What is good for the common citizen is good for all citizens, no matter their status. The way I see it, the leaders of society are the world's most prominent criminals.

CHAPTER 15

DOCTOR VISITS

I HAD YET ANOTHER APPOINTMENT WITH DR. ICEBERG. WHEN SHE asked how I'd been doing, I told her that my headaches were severe, my body pains and muscles pains and cramps had got worse, my back was hurting along with my spine, hands, and feet. I was having a hard time sleeping because of the pain. I was in pain twenty-four seven, but during the night, the pain increased unbelievably. And when the weather got cold or rainy or snowy, I would go out of my mind with pain.

I told myself that I was losing my mind with all of this pain. I had been living with for about three and a half years and, as I've said, I was worried about the future. Dr. Iceberg asked if I was seeing therapist Fay. I said yes. She asked if I had been taking my prescriptions. I said I'd been taking some but not others. I wasn't taking the psychological drugs. I was taking ibuprofen for most pain. When the pain got too bad to handle, I would take Vidicon and the muscle relaxer Flexeril. Those drugs knocked me out for two days because I was sensitive to the medicine. The sensitivity was increased because my fibromyalgia affected the receptors in my brain and the way they reacted with the drugs. Dr. Iceberg told me that, if I didn't take the psychological drugs, there was nothing more she could do for me. I told her that I was having enough problems with the Vidicon and Flexeril. I didn't want to use the other drugs because I didn't know how I would react to them. I told her she was a crazy doctor. My problems were turning into physical problems; they were not only mental at that point. I asked her why she hadn't sent me to a pain management doctor. She only avoided my question. I asked her what she was trying to do to me by not sending me to other doctors who could help me out medically, legally, and personally. I told her that my father and brother both had mesothelioma, and I asked her to test me to see if I also had it. She said I didn't have it. Then I told her that she had prescribed Zantac for my stomach pains and gas, and I had taken it for a while but then it had been recalled because it was potentially carcinogenic. I asked if she was going to test me for side effects from Zantac. She told me that my x-rays showed no cancer, but those x-rays were over a year old. I told her that my brother had been diagnosed only recently, and I had worked construction all of my life. Didn't she think I should be tested for mesothelioma? She said no, I was fine. I turned around and said, "Dr. Iceberg, do you really not care about all your patients, or do you just not care about me?" She merely said she would see me in six months. As I left her office, I realized that she was useless as a doctor, and I wanted to report her to the medical board. I started avoiding office visits with Dr. Iceberg, only going there when I needed to. I couldn't leave this doctor because my attorney had advised me that "doctor shopping" could be used against people in court cases.

That same week, I had an appointment with therapist Fay. When I got to the office, I had to fill out another computer questionnaire before I could talk to her. When I was finished, she accessed my questionnaire and explained that my answers indicated that I wasn't getting any better. I asked what she meant, and she said that I was "bottoming out" on the questionnaire. I asked what she meant. She said it suggested that I was destined to commit suicide or I would hurt the people I felt had hurt me. I told her she was nuts! I told her there was too much money involved in my lawsuits, and I wasn't about to go to jail for the dumb action of hurting someone or myself.

I asked her what she saw in that questionnaire that gave her that conclusion! Did she think I would hurt or kill someone? Fay avoided the questions. I was asked multiple times in the questionnaire if I would hurt myself or someone else. I always answered no! So, I asked her where she was getting her information. She said she had been seeing me for about a year and a half, and the questionnaire had always predicted that I would hurt myself and others. I told her how sorry I was that she was letting the results of a questionnaire decide my fate. I told her that, if I was a killer, I wouldn't be seeking help! I wouldn't care about a lawsuit, and I wouldn't be fighting with everybody to prove that the town had acted illegally. So that meant that her questionnaire was a hundred percent wrong! I asked if she had been told to take those actions. I said, "Okay, I'm leaving because your mind is made up, and that is fine." I walked out of the office and went home. I told my mother and other family members about Dr. Chow and therapist Fay Pain and how bad things were going with these professional people.

The next day, someone knocked on the door. I opened the door to see a Butland policeman on my porch. I asked what I could do for him, and he asked if I was Vincent D'Angelo. I said I was. My mother was standing at the top of the stairs listening. The officer said that he needed to take me to the hospital "under section 12." I asked what that meant. He said it meant that an official person—a doctor or therapist—had set up a section 12 because he or she believed that I might hurt myself or someone else. I asked what would happen to me if I didn't want to go. He said I would be put under protective custody, and officers would take me forcibly to the hospital. He said it would be better if I went on my own. I asked what name was on the papers, and he said there were two—Fay Pain and Dr. Kill. I told him I had never seen Dr. Kill.

So, I was escorted by the police to an ambulance and then taken to the hospital in Weymouth. When I was in the ambulance, I started to think, and then I started to get angry. These professional doctors had lied to initiate a section 12. When the ambulance got to the hospital, security guards were sent to guard me. They put me in a room where I would be observed by doctors and nurses, and this only brought out more anger within my mind. But I had to act in a responsible way. I wasn't going to feed into their dirty tactics; I would behave myself. But I was distraught over all these new problems instigated by Fay Pain.

Meanwhile, my mother drove to the hospital after she called my brothers and sister to tell them what had happened. They couldn't believe what had happened just because I had been seeking help for stress-related problems.

When the doctor came to talk with me about eight hours later, he asked me if I would hurt myself or anyone else. I said that I wouldn't. He asked why I was so upset at that moment, and I told him that I had been set up for failure. He asked what I meant, and I told him that I had been seeing a therapist, Fay Pain, and she had been telling me that she was going to section me because the questionnaire indicated that I wasn't getting better. The doctor asked if I was sure she had said this, and I said yes. I told him about my two cases against the town of Butland, and I said that I had been seeing a therapist for stress-related issues caused by my job and my medical and legal problems. I explained a bit about my medical conditions. The officers, doctors, and nurses all said that I didn't seem like a person who would hurt himself or others.

I asked the doctor if he thought I going to hurt myself or anyone, and he said he didn't think I had the characteristics of a harmful person. He said that there was a major problem if this therapist was making evaluations only on the basis of a questionnaire and no other evaluation. He asked if I had ever seen Dr. Kill, and I said no. He said that, in his opinion, other than the fact that I was upset because of the fraudulent section 12, he, as the attending doctor, and the other members of the medical staff felt that I was medically clear. They didn't believe that I had any mental problems that would incite me to hurt anyone, including myself. He said that my therapist should be reported to the authorities, and he asked if I had an attorney. When I said yes, he advised me to call him and tell him what had happened. Medically, he cleared me from the allegations.

I left the hospital with my mother, and we talked about this new problem in the car. When we got home, my brothers and sister were there. Joseph asked who had started the procedure, and I said it was my therapist and a PhD I had never even seen. Anthony said that was medical neglect by a therapist and a doctor. My mother said that what had happened was all over the town of Butland. People had been busy with their wagging tongues. I blamed the town of Butland for these problems along with my doctors and attorneys who had misled the judges in my court cases.

My sister, Sarah, told me I should report my situation to law enforcement, the attorney general's office in Rhode Island, the district attorney in Norfolk County, and news media. I told her I had tried that route, but I had received no results. These problems were breaking down my trust in this world and professional people. Even the doctor at the hospital advised me to report what was going on, as did the Butland police officer. My brother Joseph said it was crazy that professional people could see that something was wrong but they were doing nothing to help me. Sarah said that, even when most professional people know that other professionals are wrong, they don't step forward to report or complain. My brother Anthony asked if I was going to call Attorney Moakley, and I said I would do it the next day.

I soon met with Attorney Moakley, and I explained that I had been subjected to a section 12 and that Dr. Kill and therapist Fay were behind it. The Butland police had carried it out and taken me to the hospital. He said he could hardly believe it, and he didn't know why this was happening to me. But he promised he would find out why. The sad thing is, however, that Moakley never took the time to understand or look into my misfortune at the hands of medical professionals. He told me that he needed the records from the hospital and the therapist. He asked if I would be going back to therapist Fay. I told him no way! She had betrayed me and violated my rights, and I had many other issues with her as well. Moakley said he didn't blame me, but we needed someone to speak on my behalf with regard to my medical records. I said that there must be way to involve an independent doctor in my case. He said that was a possibility, but would be expensive, and he would me to add to his retainer. I asked how much more, and he said $10,000. I agreed and wrote out a check. I told him that any new doctor would have to understand fibromyalgia and stress-related problems. He told me not to worry; he would take care of finding an independent doctor. He said we needed someone who could piece together the puzzle of my medical records to make both my law suits stronger. He told me to give him a few days, and he'd call me when he had news. Eventually, Attorney Moakley contacted three doctors. I would have to visit the first two in person for evaluation. The first doctor would charge me $20,000, and the second, $15,000. The third doctor was Allen's friend, and they had worked together in the past. He would charge me only $3,000 to look over my records and make evaluations without having to see me in person.

I asked Moakley which was the best choice. He said that the first doctor dealt with fibromyalgia and stress-related problems, but I would have to go to New York two or three times to see him. The third doctor would look over my records and give his opinion without seeing me. He was the least expensive, and he had worked with Moakley in the past. I decided to go with the third doctor, Dr. Grossman, and I asked how long it would take him to go over my records. Moakley said about a month. I got my hospital records from the hospital in Weymouth and sent them to Moakley. He requested my records from therapist Fay and received them two weeks later.

CHAPTER 16

DR. ORLANDO AND THE CENTERS FOR DISEASE CONTROL AND PREVENTION

W<small>HEN</small> I <small>STARTED RESEARCHING MY MEDICAL PROBLEMS AND</small> conditions, I came across the website of the Centers for Disease Control and Prevention (CDC). This component of the Department of Health and Human is dedicated to using science and available data to keep Americans healthy. The agency shares its information worldwide and shares guidelines with governments and medical professionals. Recently, the CDC took a leadership role during the 2020 corona virus (COVID-19) pandemic.

The CDC investigates any new medical issues that arise worldwide. I found a great deal of information on the CDC website about fibromyalgia, IBS, and other stress-related medical problems. I printed out this information and sent it to Attorney Moakley and my doctors.

What happened to me from this point forward was just an unbelievable nightmare that affected my health, my legal battles; indeed, it affected my entire life.

People who are over fifty years old and suffer from stress-related conditions are more likely to have heart attacks and strokes. Stress causes physical and mental reactions. Physical reactions include general aches and pains, chest pain, exhaustion, trouble sleeping, headaches, dizziness, shaking, high blood pressure, muscle tension, jaw clenching, stomach or digestive problems, sexual dysfunction, and a weakened immune system. Mental reactions include anxiety, irritability, depression, panic attacks, sadness, and mental confusion.

People who try to fix things on their own are likely to find themselves drinking too much, smoking too much, using drugs, gambling, overeating or developing an eating disorder, or engaging in compulsive sex or excess shopping or Internet browsing. Conditions like fibromyalgia and IBS can make these symptoms worse.

Drugs provide very little help for these conditions; they can become yet another problem if patients become addicted to them. Nervous system malfunctions and chemical changes in the body can even lead to suicide. My pain alone could have been enough to drive me to suicide, especially since it had gone on for seven years.

Irritable bowel syndrome (IBS) symptoms include abdominal pain, bloating, diarrhea, and constipation. One doctor told me that my intestines were continually contracting and relaxing in my abdominal cavity, and that was causing both constipation or diarrhea. My anxiety was increased because I was always worried that I might have an embarrassing accident if I couldn't find a toilet when I need one. Abnormalities in the nerves of the digestive system may cause patients to experience significant discomfort when their abdomen stretches because of gas or stool.

Once I began to experience stress, IBS and fibromyalgia took over my life and left me nearly helpless. I tried to notify the proper authorities—doctors, attorneys, law enforcement officials, and judges—about Robert Smith's criminal actions, but no one stepped up to help me, and that made my symptoms worse.

The CDC website provided me with a lot of information about my health issues, and I thought it could also could help me resolve my medical and legal problems. When I approached my attorney and my doctors and, finally, the judges with what I thought was help, I received absolutely no gratitude. They made me feel that I had done something wrong by doing all my hard work and passing the information along to them. I had proved that I was a brilliant man, and I had taken the time to look up all the information without any assistance from doctors, attorneys, or judges. Remember, all these professional people had as many as seven to eleven years of college, and I outshone all of them with my knowledge and information, both medical and legal. I'd had a problem all my life because I always took the time and spent the effort to know all I could about my carpentry, truck driving, medical issues, legal issues, and just about everything else I was involved in. The people I was dealing with did not like dealing with me; I was a danger to them because I was the better man and more intelligent.

I went to see Attorney Moakley. I usually had a family member with me during all my legal and medical appointments, and I did on this day as well. I told Moakley about all of the medical and legal research I had been doing, and I showed him the printouts that I had prepared for him. He looked at them and explained that the information would do nothing to help the legal side of the cases. My family member and I couldn't believe it; I asked him what he was talking about. I had laid it all out for him and my doctors. He said that the information might be helpful to the doctors, but it wasn't for him. He reminded me that he had told me that he could use medical information only from the doctors and not from me, even though I'd found it on the Internet.

Moakley said that the best information had come from our independent consultant, Dr. Eric Grossman. His report was favorable to my legal position. In addition, Moakley and Dr. Grossman had

had a phone conversation about the cases, and Dr. Grossman had said that he couldn't believe that the doctors in Rhode Island were not cooperating with Attorney Moakley or the courts. He felt it was unheard of for doctors or any other professional to act that way. My attorney gave me a copy of Dr. Grossman's report and said he would also hand it in to the courts.

I was upset that my attorney would not accept my research. He said anyone could look up that information on the Internet. I asked him what he had been doing in the way of investigation and discovery.

He assured me that he was gathering information, so I asked him where *his* paperwork was. He just avoided my request and talked around in endless circles. I told him I needed tangible evidence that we could prove in a courtroom. I asked him if he had put up an argument with the town representatives about the town attorney's information. Once again, he talked in circles and provided no answers. I knew that he was not doing his job properly. I saw this as a breach of contract between attorney and client. I told him that my mind and body were getting better. I had looked up more information and talked to another attorney for advice. Moakley listened without replying. Then I started to challenge him and anyone else who would lie about me or provide false information relating to these cases.

I had an appointment with Dr. Orlando, the rheumatologist. I gave him the information I had collected from the Internet and other places. He looked through the articles and asked me what I wanted him to do with them. I told him that, for a start, he could look at the report from Dr. Grossman stating that I was disabled because of all my health conditions. He said he didn't take reports from other doctors; he made his own conclusions. I told him that Dr. Grossman's report was information that he should have about my health conditions. He said that he had information from the doctors within the hospital system that I belonged to and the other doctors I had been seeing. I told him that, with only that information in play, I was being set up for failure by the hospital system and the doctors. I then asked him why he hadn't complied with the requests of my attorney and the other doctors to share my records.

Dr. Orlando said that my attorney hadn't requested records from him after he had requested them once at the beginning of the cases. When I asked him when that was, he said it had been about three years ago. When I asked if Attorney Moakley had requested updated records more recently, he said no. I asked if the same thing was happening with my other doctors, and he told me that my records were all in the computer system, and if anyone ignored them or disregarded them, I would have to handle the problem myself. I asked him to write up my diagnosis and prognosis including information about all my health conditions. Dr. Orlando said that I needed to have my attorney ask for that report. I asked him to write it up for me right then while I waited; I would deliver it to my attorney. But Dr. Orlando said no. I would have to go through my attorney. He then said we were done, and he walked out of the room. My family member and I walked out of the office. We had all sorts of questions about the doctor's explanation. We asked each other what was going on with all these professional doctors and others who were not doing their jobs properly. No one seemed to be helping me.

CHAPTER 17

DR. ICEBERG, ATTORNEY MOAKLEY, THE SOCIAL SECURITY OFFICE, AND MY FAMILY

IT WAS TIME ONCE AGAIN TO VISIT DR. ICEBERG, AND I HAD THE report from Dr. Grossman. As always, I had a family member with me in case I needed a witness in court. Dr. Iceberg came into the room and asked how I was doing. I told her my health was pretty bad, but I had news from Dr. Grossman, who had evaluated my records and concluded that I qualified for a disability. Dr. Iceberg said that she made her own evaluations; she didn't accept information from other doctors. I asked her if she would fight Dr. Orlando's disability diagnosis. She said she would. She said she was my primary care doctor, and she was the only one who could confirm or deny a diagnoses. I asked her if she was admitting that her opinions were going to hurt me and my cases, medical and legal. I reminded her that she was ignoring the opinions of another doctor within her hospital system as well as one outside her system. She said she didn't care about the opinions of other doctors. Once again, my family member and I were astonished at what we were hearing. Dr. Iceberg turned around and walked out of the office saying we were all done. She didn't even ask me any questions about my health or examine me, both of which had been the reason for that day's appointment.

I returned home and talked once again to my family members about the doctors and attorneys. No one in my family could believe what I was telling them about these professional people. They couldn't understand why this was happening to me. The professional people and agencies I had written to had ignored my letters and done nothing about the lack of action from the professional people I was dealing with. I told my family members that we need to get more efficient about the way we addressed these problems at a legal level.

Television news reports cover stories about people with mental problems who go on rampages and go crazy, hurting people for no obvious reason. Neither the news media nor the police make public the events and circumstances that led these people to act in such a frightening way. These people have problems that might not have escalated if their doctors had heard their cries for help. If they went through anything like what I was going through, I understand how they could end up being the subject of a news story. I don't believe in committing crimes or acts violence; I do believe in getting help. But when authorities don't help, people are the losers all the way around.

I had too much to lose. I didn't want to jeopardize my cases by doing anything illegal in public or private, and I refused to go to jail for the wrong reasons. My family members agreed that I was doing the right thing by reporting to law enforcement and anyone who would listen. Still, the problem was that nobody wanted to hear the truth about the dirty systems of law, medicine, and government in our country. The professional people were breaking the law and getting away with doing so. These laws had been introduced by politicians and law enforcement, and people in various positions of power were able to break or manipulate the laws to fit their crimes so that they didn't have to go to jail or pay in any way for the dirty deeds that they committed.

I retreated to my music, which helped me so much. It helped me to relax and think. It calmed my emotions and provided me with energy when I was down. I also relaxed by playing mind games on my phone—crossword puzzles, spelling games, math games, and anything that made me use my brain. They provided me with a break from my health and legal problems. This reminds me of the movie *What About Bob?* with Richard Dreyfuss and Bill Murray. Dreyfuss plays a therapist who advises his patient, played by Murray, to take a vacation from his problems. I was taking mini vacations with my music and my mind puzzles—a much better strategy than recreational drugs or alcohol or gambling. I would never do anything that would hurt me, my people, or the laws.

The most important thing to me was to figure out how to find a way to prove my cases to the proper authorities. I got away now and then with my girlfriend, Lisa, for dinner or a movie; it was nice to spend time with her. I also tried to do things around the house like cleaning, cooking, food shopping, taking showers, cutting the grass, and shoveling snow, but as time went on, my symptoms made these everyday tasks more difficult. If felt as if my days of having fun were over. I had to do everything at a slow pace, and I had to be very smart to outwit the professional people and report them so I could get justice.

Attorney Moakley had explained that I should apply to Social Security for Supplemental Security Income (SSI), which is paid to people who have disabilities or for other reasons. I thought that applying would interfere with the cases, but he said it wouldn't. He said that what would happen would depend on the SSI benefits I might receive. For example, if I received $500 a week from my job and I received SSI in the amount of $500 a month, I would lose one week of pay from my job. I asked him why I should make it easier for the town. They would have to pay me less every week. I asked why the federal government should have to pay for a problem that was caused by the town. He told me that was what I should do for income. I told him there were rules that governed SSI payments. The first rule was that there would be a limit on the amount in my bank account. The second rule was that, when I received a settlement, my SSI benefits would stop until the settlement money was used up, and I would have to keep receipts to prove where the money went. If the Social Security Administration (SSA) didn't approve of something I bought with my settlement money, they would not reinstall the benefits. I told him that was a lose-lose situation. But he told me that, if I succeeded in getting SSI benefits, I would have a better chance of winning the cases. Then I asked if the doctors who were not cooperating me or with him would cooperate with the SSA in my effort to secure benefits. He said I was just trying to confuse my problems, so I finally agreed to apply to the Social Security Administration for SSI. We would see what would happen.

I went to the Social Security office to apply for SSI. The person I talked to said that processing my application would take about three months. If, for some reason, I was denied, I could file an appeal through that office. If the appeal was denied, I would go before a judge in Sealand, Rhode Island. If that failed, I could appeal to the SSI Administrative office in Washington DC. If that failed, the last step would be Superior Court. I started the process and waited to hear from the Social Security Office.

Three months later, I was denied, and I went to the office to file an appeal. The person who helped with my appeal said that we would see if the doctors had changed my health status. I told him that my doctors were not cooperating with the Social Security Administration, and he said that's what it looked like to him too—no cooperation.

Once again, I was denied SSI benefits. I would have to go to the Brock office to file papers, and then I would see the judge in the Sealand office.

The day came for my SSI court session with Judge Hare; this was my third appeal, and I was alone this time without a family member. I had to check in and prove who I was and that I had an appointment with the judge. I had never been there before, and the process was a challenge for me with all my health issues. The anxiety hit me first; I was so nervous to be at the SSI office. When they called to go in front of the judge, my anxiety kicked into high gear. My stomach started to cramp up, and my fibromyalgia pain was killing me. The clerk had come to get me; she explained that I would be speaking to one of the best judges at that office. She asked if I had the records that had been sent to me. I told her I did, but everything was on a compact disc, and I couldn't open it. She said she would print out the paperwork for me. I had seen how big my folder was at the Brock office. I went in front of the judge, and he and explained all the court's procedures.

Judge Hare asked if I had an attorney with me, and I said no. The judge said he would telephone an independent job advisor to help with the information about my job; she would make sure the legal side of the case was in order. The judge explained the case to the advisor and answered her questions related to my health problems. He told her that I had anxiety issues, IBS, fibromyalgia, and other stress-related problems. He asked her if I was fit to work, and she said no. Then he asked her if I was capable of working. The advisor said no, not with all those medical problems. The judge asked if I could work standing, sitting, or walking. The advisor said that I couldn't work under any conditions, and she added that my situation would only worsen if he had problems getting SSI. The advisor also said that any company's insurance company would have a problem with the company employing someone with illnesses like mine. Judge Hare thanked her, ended the call, and told me he would notify me by mail with a decision in about three months.

Every time I received information, I passed it on to Attorney Moakley via email or fax, so I could prove that I had sent it. He knew about SSI application process and how I had been denied the first two times.

After four months, I received a notice in the mail from the Social Security Administration. I opened the envelope and found that I had been denied for the third time. The judge explained that I could work at three different types of jobs, but the jobs weren't available in the area of Sealand or even Rhode Island. The next step was to appeal to the SSI Administrative office in Washington DC. I filled out the papers and sent them to Washington knowing that I would not hear a decision for an entire year. Meanwhile, I called Attorney Moakley and told him about my third denial. I didn't understand. The judge had heard the job advisor clarify three different times that I could not return to work. Also she had said that insurance companies didn't like companies hiring people with so many health issues. Moakley told me to go on to the next step and see what happened.

In a phone call, I told Attorney Moakley that my medical records weren't clear enough for the judges to make a proper decision. I said we needed more detailed information to prove how poor my health had become. I told him that my doctors were holding out and not recording the detailed information that would explain how bad my health was then and how it would get worse over time. I said that I had given him those details, but he had refused to use them. He said he couldn't do anything for me. The SSI personnel made their decisions according to people's medical records. He, as my lawyer, couldn't help.

I told him things were going wrong with my cases because he was withholding the detailed information that could bring about a favorable decision. I told him I didn't care about SSI, and I reminded him that I believed that, if I received SSI, the town would get off easier when it came to upholding their responsibilities. He told me that the papers I had given him would never be considered evidence by any court. I said I was standing alone. I had made sure that my research information had gone to him, and I expected he would pass it along to the right people. Before we hung up, I knew that he was pissed off with me for going above his head for justice.

Time passed, and I received a notice from Washington DC. The judge said he could only have made a positive judgment on my claim if he had detailed information about my diagnosis and prognosis. Without all the proper papers, he had no option but to deny my appeal. He stated that my appeal had been a waste of everybody's time.

Once again, I contacted Attorney Moakley. In an email, I explained the information I received with my SSI denial. He said the same thing—it wasn't his problem. I told him we had to have detailed medical records in order to win both cases. He just ignored me. Later in the day, I received an email from him. He was letting me know that the depositions for the discrimination case were coming up. The first one would be at the office of Gram Stoneman. The second would be at the Holiday Inn in Mansfield. I emailed and asked about our witnesses, but he never answered. I was fighting a losing battle with doctors, attorneys, witnesses, former employers. Soon I would be fighting with judges. Plus, I still had received no responses to the letters that I had been writing to the legal authorities complaining about the crimes of the medical and legal professionals.

CHAPTER 18

FIRST DISCRIMINATION
CASE DEPOSITION

O<small>N</small> S<small>EPTEMBER</small> 24, 2018, I <small>ATTENDED THE FIRST DEPOSITION IN MY</small> discrimination case at the BFY law office in Sealand, Rhode Island. The meeting was to start at nine in the morning, but Attorney Moakley was late, which made me angry because he had told me to arrive early! He had not taken the time to prepare me for this meeting as most attorneys would. I showed up with a family member for support because I was not able to drive because of my physical illnesses.

I told my brother that I was nervous because I had never done anything like that before. Then I started to experience anxiety and stress problems. I worried because Attorney Moakley hadn't shown up, which made my symptoms worse. He finally arrived more than half an hour late. When I asked him why he was late, he blamed the trains and buses. I told him to catch earlier trains and busses, but he ignored me and told me we should check in. I asked him why he hadn't prepared me for the meeting, and he just told me, "It's too late now." I said it was way too late; it should have been done the day before. He didn't say anything.

The following people were present in the meeting: Amy Bosh, shorthand reporter for the commonwealth of Rhode Island; Gram Stoneman, town discrimination attorney; Allen Moakley, attorney for the plaintiff (me), and me, the plaintiff, Vincent D Angelo.

Attorney Stoneman would control this meeting, and Attorney Moakley would be allowed only to object to Stoneman's questions; otherwise, he had to be quiet during the depositions. Stoneman asked me to prove who I was, so I gave him my driver's license. He asked where I lived, and then backtracked, asking for information from the past up to the present time. Stoneman then asked Attorney Moakley if he had the relevant files with him. He replied that he didn't have his complete case file. Stoneman asked me if I had all my licenses, and I told him that I had given Moakley copies of them. Stoneman asked Moakley if he had them, and he said no. Stoneman asked me to tell him about my licenses. I said I had a CDL class A driver's license, a 2A hoisting license, an HVAC license, and a construction license.

The questions would go on forever, and I couldn't understand their meaning. Once Stoneman established who I was, he asked other kinds of questions that seemed ridiculous to me, an ordinary citizen. He was asking me legal questions that I didn't understand. Politicians and lawyers wrote the laws, and they are too complicated for an ordinary citizen to understand. That is shameful for a legal system and legal professionals. Legal authorities could trick an ordinary citizen into lying, and the citizen wouldn't even realize it if he or she didn't understand the law. During the deposition, I also noticed that the procedure was on a one-way track because neither my attorney nor the judge was questioned or cross-examined by Stoneman.

After a while, I asked for a break. I wanted a chance to complain to Moakley about the way the deposition was going. Stoneman gave us the use of the room for a private talk. I wanted to talk to Moakley to see what he could do to obtain better results if possible. He told me that these depositions provided an opportunity for judges to rule out insignificant cases and save citizens' tax money. I said that the case was related to the town of Butland first, not to the people. I said that's a lie the judges tell the politicians when they waste money on everything else in our country. I asked Moakley why he hadn't brought my file as other attorneys would do for their clients and themselves. He said he had forgotten them. I told him I was trusting him with my life and I had given him a lot of money. I said, "This is how you take care of my case and me?" I told him it was common legal practice for a lawyer to be prepared with his client's complete records. I told him I found it unbelievable that he had "forgotten" them. I told him that his handling of my entire case had been incompetent. I asked him if the town was paying him to "throw" the case. Moakley didn't answer that question. I asked how much more we would miss because he didn't have my records.

I also told him that the deposition was a joke because Stoneman had control, and there was no judge to witness the actions of this attorney. A judge would see only words on a piece of paper, and they would have little meaning. I didn't even understand how a judge could glean pertinent information and a decision from documents like these depositions. Without the physical interaction in a courtroom, what good were those papers? Stoneman was picking only questions that were set against me; there was no judge or attorney to form opinions or ask questions.

The documents didn't show the badgering, the improper questions, or the attorneys' demeanor with witnesses and me. Plus, my own attorney hadn't even bothered to bring my records. The deposition was not stopped because the records were not available. I felt that the absence of records could lead to malpractice charges against both attorneys. Allen avoid my questions as much as possible, and he didn't take the hint when I mentioned stopping the deposition because he wasn't prepared with the proper records. I told him he hadn't done his job. He hadn't advised correctly from the start. I also said that Stoneman realized that Moakley was an incompetent attorney. Either that or my attorney had been paid to "forget" my records. That they were not present certainly gave Stoneman the edge over us. I told Allen I needed ten minutes to calm myself so I could continue with these improper proceedings. He left me alone, and ten minutes later, we all started again with more questions.

The next questions were about me being sick at the end of my employment. Stoneman asked if I had turned in doctor's letters to excuse me from work when I was sick. I said I had. He asked when I had submitted the letters, and I said I always hand in the letters on the day I received them. I had received permission-to-be-out-of-work letters from my doctors three times before I was released from my job. When I was released, I was not given a reason. When I had asked Smith why he was releasing me, he wouldn't answer. Stoneman asked if I remembered what that doctor's letter said; I told him that my attorney had copies of all the letters and he should have provided them for the deposition. There was no response from Stoneman because Moakley didn't have my case records. I asked Stoneman what was the purpose of these questions. I told him they should be asked in front of a judge. I told him that the deposition was a one-way conversation or interrogation and an infringement of my rights as a citizen of this country, especially as my attorney wasn't allowed to ask any questions or correct manipulative questions. Stoneman laughed and said that this was the law at its best! I said the law was wrong because every citizen in this country has the right to be heard in front of a judge and without the influence of this interrogation of manipulation called a deposition.

Stoneman said we needed to get the deposition done that day.

He then asked if I claimed discrimination against Robert Smith and the town. I said I did. He asked if I could explain the situation that backed up my claim. I explained that one Saturday afternoon when we were working overtime, Smith came in and used the excuse that he had some work to do in the office. Instead, he started to talk to three people. I was one of them. The others were Scott, the highway foreman, and another worker, Ben Jokes. Smith had directed the conversation to Scott, but Ben and I were listening to the discussion. Smith asked why the workers were so upset with him over new contract problems in deliberation. Scott answered that it was Smith's responsibility to sign an agreement for the new contract. People depend on pay raises so they can support their families. Smith had said that he had nothing to do with the new contract, but Scott had said he did because the former superintendent, Larry Smalls, had made sure that the new contracts were always signed and completed before the deadline of July 1. At that point, we were just about a year beyond the deadline, and there was still no contract signed. Smith only pushed off this conversation and started a new conversation about a man named Todd Williams. Stoneman asked me to explain what Todd had to do with the discrimination charges. I said that Todd was a friend of mine. He was a black man and a good guy and a hard worker for the town. He worked about three jobs—part time for the school department, full time with the Butland DPW office, and part time as a constable. When Smith started talking in a discriminatory way about Todd, I took offense to his insults. Smith then started racially insulting Todd. I was even more offended because I'm Sicilian—an Italian from a Mediterranean area—and I have a bit of color to my skin too. Southern Italians and Sicilians have a skin color that is anywhere from olive to brown. When we tan from the sun, our skin can turn dark brown. Also, I am in a relationship with a woman of mixed race. For these reasons, I was insulted by Smith's comments. He showed no consideration for people of color. He just showed his ignorance. Especially in a place of business, people have no right to express racial ideas. No one of any ethnicity should have to listen to comments by ignorant people. I should be within my rights to report Smith without any consequences to me personally or to my job. Because of Smith's words and ignorance, he should face charges of racial discrimination. I would have been able to keep my job if the law had worked correctly and in the right way. Instead, I lost my job because Smith lied about me and my work. Because Smith knew that I had heard his racist comments about Todd, he had to get rid of me. It was to my benefit that there were other witnesses— Scott and Ben had both heard Smith's discriminatory words. Smith had to discredit me with false accusations so that he could fire me. He was a mean person to me and to the other workers. Because he carried the authority of his superintendent position, nobody dared to challenge him. They couldn't afford to lose their jobs at the DPW office. Smith had started to harass me more and more, threatening my job. I started to have symptoms because of anxiety caused by him. And finally he released me from my job. After that, I start getting sicker. I had been mentally abused by a man with power. He was in a winning position because of his power; he was convinced he would not be challenged by anyone at the DPW office or outside sources. He would suffer no consequences for his bad behavior.

The date of the discrimination incident was July 31, 2014. I was getting sick to my stomach at that time, but I hadn't realized until later, when I saw a therapist, that my physical reaction was a result of stress. Stoneman asked why I hadn't reported the incident to someone. I said I had just explained that I wanted to keep my job just like everybody else at a the DPW office. He asked why I was complaining now. I said that Smith was trying to cover up his own faults, and he was making false allegations that I was a bad worker. This led to me losing my job. After that I had no choice but to complain about a discriminating boss and a bully! I turned the situation around, making it against Smith. I especially wanted revenge for his racial comments about Todd. I explained that Smith would have been better off leaving me alone after the racial remarks, but he pushed me till I started getting sick, and after I got sick, he released me from my job without any cause. Legally, an employer must give a reason for dismissing an employee. Smith had broken that law, and the town of Butland was upholding his decision. I asked both Stoneman and Moakley if it mattered to either of them that Smith had broken another law. They both just avoided the question. I then declared that the questions that were being asked at that deposition weren't about determining the truth; they were only to find out how they could all cheat me out of justice and help Smith and the town win the battle. I said that the government upheld unfair regulations and laws that favored criminals like Stoneman and Moakley.

Stoneman continued questioning me and asked if I had written any letters. I said I had written many letters of complaint, and I named a few recipients. Stoneman showed me a letter and asked me read it out loud. As I began reading, I realized that it wasn't one of the letters I had written. It had been written by somebody within the town of Butland who knew about my cases and was trying to help me by proving that the town had been wrong to dismiss me. The letter stated that Smith's accusations suggesting poor work on my part were lies. There was no signature on the paper. When I told Stoneman I had not written that letter, he became frustrated that he had introduced evidence that might go in my favor rather than the town's. And the court recorder had permanently recorded the entire exchange.

Then Stoneman brought up my experiences with the Social Security Administration Supplemental Security Income (SSI) applications. I asked him what that had to do with his side of the case because it didn't prove any fault between the town and me. Attorney Moakley asked me to leave the office so he and Stoneman could go off the record to discuss whether my information from the Social Security Administration should be part of the disposition. Finally, Stoneman called me back and said that they would not use that information. Then Stoneman announced that we were all done with my deposition, and we could all go home. But I wanted to talk to Moakley before we left.

As Attorney Moakley and I left the building, I asked why he hadn't done more for me and my case. I told him he had merely copied the discrimination board information from my first attorney, Bob Keyhole. He hadn't written any complaint information himself. We were working on two cases—one with the discrimination board and one with the US district court. Each venue had different rules. I asked what would happen if the information he copied wasn't completely correct. I said Stoneman had based his questioning on that original paperwork, so now to the case was all wrong; I had also said this to Attorney Keyhole when I lost the discrimination board hearing. I told Moakley that he'd better start doing his job as an attorney, or there would be legal consequences for him. I would not hesitate to report his improper handling of my two cases to the authorities. I told him I'd never been afraid of a fight, legal or otherwise. I said I was already fighting doctors, Smith, the town, and the town attorney. I could add him to that list with no problem.

CHAPTER 19

SECOND DISCRIMINATION CASE DEPOSITION

On October 3, 2018, I attended the second deposition in my discrimination case. The new superintendent of the DPW office, Jimmy Flynn, and retired superintendent, Robert Smith, would be present. Flynn would be interviewed first at ten in the morning, and Smith would be interviewed just after lunch. As usual, I showed up early, and Attorney Moakley was nowhere to be found. Again, Moakley was late for a scheduled meeting, and his office was around the corner from Holiday Inn where the deposition was taking pace. When he did show up, I asked what I should expect at the day's depositions. He said I would hear Flynn's and Smith's depositions. I asked what had happened to the list of people he had requested as witnesses on my behalf. He made up the excuse that they would not come forward for fear of losing their jobs. Also, I didn't have the money to continue the depositions. He said it would be a waste of money if the town urged witnesses to lie about me so they could keep their jobs. That was one way to free the town from any wrongful doings. I realized that I was fighting a losing battle. Without truth, there would be no justice. I asked Moakley why Flynn was there; he had not been my boss. He said that Flynn had been there when I worked there, and now he was the new superintendent. I told him that Flynn had never interacted with me other than saying hello or good-bye. He just said that we would see what his story was. He told me to be quiet during the depositions or I'd be kicked out. He told me to write down any questions I might have and give them to him so he could ask them.

We were about to begin. Present were Brenda Roth, court reporter; Gram Stoneman, attorney for the town of Butland; Jimmy Flynn, new superintendent of the DPW office, Vincent D Angelo, plaintiff; and Allen Moakley, attorney for the plaintiff. Moakley asked if Smith would be there that day, and Stoneman said he would. Moakley asked Flynn for a license to prove his identity for the record. Then he asked Flynn to talk about his professional history up to the present. He asked Flynn if he had gone to college, and Flynn said he had. He asked what courses he had taken, and Flynn said he had a BS degree in civil engineering.

Then Moakley asked how Flynn had met me. Flynn said he had met me at my initial job interview with the town of Butland, when I was hired. He asked if others had been present at that meeting, and Flynn said there were three people besides me. He named Superintendent Robert Smith and himself, but he couldn't remember who the other attendee had been. Moakley asked if he remembered Assistant Supervisor Chuck Freedman, and Flynn said he didn't. Moakley asked what he knew about me and my job. Flynn said that all the foremen had been complaining about my performance at work. When Moakley asked for these men's names, Flynn listed Moe Dirt, Joe Heap, and Jeff Knowles. Moakley asked if that was all, and Flynn said there had been seven foremen in the DPW office. When Moakley asked for the names of the other foremen, Flynn said he couldn't remember. Moakley asked if Flynn was the new acting superintendent. When Flynn said yes, Moakley expressed surprise that he didn't know their names. Flynn just repeated that he didn't remember their names. Moakley asked if Flynn knew of any complaints from Smith when he was in office. Flynn said he didn't remember. Moakley asked how reliable the foremen's stories were, and Flynn said very reliable. When Moakley asked what sort of complaints people were expressing about my work, Flynn said he didn't remember.

Moakley offered to help Flynn remember what I had been doing when Flynn was an assistant supervisor only four years back. He asked where the new workers started working—in what department? Flynn said the sanitation department. Moakley asked how long they usually remained in that job before they were moved up in position. Flynn said when a new job opened up or one year later after the probation period. Moakley asked if a new job had opened up for me. Flynn said no. I had worked only in the sanitation department. Moakley asked if that meant that I was always on the garbage trucks with two other workers. Flynn said yes. So Moakley asked him how could the other foremen see me at work in order to come up with their complaints. He asked if those foremen were working on the garbage trucks. Flynn said no, and Moakley asked him how he could verify the truth of the foremen's complaints. Flynn went back to saying he didn't remember. Moakley asked if Flynn had witnessed me doing anything wrong at the DPW office, and Flynn, true to form, said he didn't remember.

Moakley asked "Then why are you here? Were you told to lie about Vince and his job?" Stoneman objected to these questions. Moakley responded to Stoneman saying that Flynn didn't have any answers, and it appeared that someone had programmed him to tell lies. Stoneman was quiet after that. Moakley asked if he could continue with his questioning, and Stoneman said yes. Moakley said that we might need to have the seven foremen come in for depositions so we could find out the truth. If Flynn's statement was incorrect, he would be guilty of perjury. Stoneman got upset and asked for a break to talk to Flynn; Moakley said okay. So Moakley and I left the room, and we had our talk about this situation. He said that Flynn had had no idea about what was going on with this questioning or his job, and whether the complaints about me were true or not. I told him that I had been handing him notes that said he was lying. Flynn had never been around except in the morning to pass out the work orders. Occasionally we saw him around the work yard or the office. Moakley said that was good for us; I said Smith's statements would be just as bad if not worse than Flynn's.

We all returned to the table and proceed with the questioning, which now focused on me getting sick. Moakley asked what rules employees had to follow when they got sick. Flynn said they had to get a doctor's letter to excuse them from work. Moakley asked if I had provided these letters. Flynn said yes. Moakley asked if this rule was in the handbook given to Butland employees. Flynn said yes. Then Moakley asked why I had been released from my job. Flynn said it was for work performance. Moakley asked what that meant. I had been on the back of a garbage truck throwing trash all day. How could a person make mistakes with that job? Flynn admitted it would be difficult. Moakley asked him to describe my performance; Flynn said he couldn't. Moakley asked him again if he'd been sent there to lie about me. Flynn had no answer.

Stoneman again objected to the line of questioning; Moakley told him that something was wrong. Then he said we would talk to Robert Smith. Stoneman agreed. While we waited for Smith, Moakley and I stepped aside to talk about Flynn's statement. I asked him if he believed me that people who had power in the town were lying about me. He said that something was going on within the town, but we had no proof. I said that there was proof, but it was vanishing before our eyes.

Robert Smith was the second witness and the town of Butland defendant. After establishing that Smith was who he claimed to be, Moakley asked what high school he had attended. Smith said Butland High School. He had graduated in 1969. Moakley asked if he'd gone to college. Smith said no. He had started working at the Butland DPW office right out of high school. Moakley asked how long he had worked there. Smith said from 1969 to 2015. Then he retired. Moakley asked why he had retired, and Smith said his health had been failing. Moakley asked if there was any another reason, and Smith said no, but he said it with an attitude. Next, Moakley asked what his first position had been at the DPW office. Smith said that he had started as a laborer and advanced to truck driver, heavy equipment operator, foreman, assistant supervisor, and finally superintendent. Moakley observed that Smith had actually grown up with the DPW office and then achieved power as a superintendent. He had spent all his life in Butland. Smith said yes. Next, Moakley asked if Smith had had any problems or if anyone had complained about him during all his years with the DPW office. Smith said no. Moakley asked if he would find evidence of problems or complaints if he looked into Smith's record. Smith said he wouldn't. Moakley reminded him that lying during a deposition was perjury, but Smith did not retract his answer.

Moakley asked Smith how he knew me, and Smith explained that I had first been a snowplowing subcontractor for the town. Moakley asked how long I had been a subcontractor, and Smith said he didn't remember exactly, but maybe ten years before he hired me for full-time employment with the town. Moakley said he could help Smith with his memory. He asked if Smith remembered a day back in 2002 and a brand-new blue Ford pickup F-250 series with an eight-foot plow blade. Smith said he didn't. Moakley asked what the requirements were for plowing. Smith said he wanted 250 trucks or bigger with eight-foot or bigger plows. Moakley asked if

Smith remembered me asking for two separate applications—one for contract plowing and one for full-time employment. Smith said he didn't. Moakley asked if he remembered a conversation with me about my new truck and how plowing the streets of Butland could ruin it. Smith said he didn't remember. Moakley asked if Smith checked the equipment of new contractors before plowing season to make sure they met his requirements. Smith said he didn't. Moakley asked if Smith remembered any man asking for two applications, and Smith said he didn't. Moakley asked why he had hired me as a town employee. Smith said I was an excellent snowplow driver, and he thought I would be an asset to the DPW office. Moakley asked, if I had been a good worker, what had changed to make him say I was a bad worker? Smith said he didn't know.

Moakley accused Smith of being a superintendent who didn't know what was going on under his own leadership. Smith said that he relied on the assistant supervisors and the foremen to relay necessary information. Moakley asked what happened when these people lied about situations or didn't know what was going on. Smith said he would have incorrect or incomplete information. Moakley asked again why he believed that I was a bad worker. Smith said he'd got the information from his leaders. Moakley asked if he ever checked up on those people to make sure their information was correct. Smith said he didn't; he believed in his leaders. Moakley suggested that they could have lied, and Smith said it could have happened, but he trusted his leaders and himself. Moakley asked what my position was when I was hired. Smith said I had been hired as a laborer and truck driver. I had been placed with the sanitation department. Moakley asked Smith if my job had changed over the years before I was dismissed. Smith said it hadn't; I was still in the sanitation department. Moakley asked how I could foul up the job of throwing trash all day. Smith said he didn't know. Moakley asked if he was the boss of the office, didn't he have control over everything? Smith said no. Stoneman jumped in to object. Moakley told Stoneman that the answers that Smith had provide proved that the entire case was a joke. Smith didn't know anything about his own office or his supervisory staff or his workers. Stoneman said we needed a break.

Moakley and I left the room so we could talk about Smith's deposition. Moakley said that Smith never knew what was going on in his office, and he was lying with every answer he gave. He said that neither Smith nor Flynn ever took the time to find out for sure if there was any truth about the issues surrounding my employment. He said it sounded as if they were making up a story built on lies. I told Moakley that we needed to take this controversy to a courtroom so we could hear statements from other witnesses who worked for the town. I knew their testimony would not cost me any money. I said that both Smith and Flynn were lying about their stories. I had been passing notes to Moakley throughout their statements. I praised Moakley for asking specific questions that tripped both Flynn and Smith up in obvious lies. I told him they were both guilty of perjury, and we should be able to use the recording against them, the town, and the town attorney. Moakley told me I was getting too far ahead of myself; we needed to finish the depositions first. Then, we could address further actions when we received the transcripts. I asked him again about the list of witnesses I had given him. Moakley reminded me that they wouldn't come forth willingly because that would jeopardize their jobs. Also, I was running out of money. As Moakley and I went back to the room, I wondered if he was trying to get more money from me. Money was just another problem for me.

When we returned to the deposition table, Moakley asked Smith if he had ever had a private conversation with me when he asked me to spy on the men at the DPW office. Smith said he didn't remember. Moakley asked if he had ever told me that I could trust him and there were men he couldn't trust. Again, Smith couldn't remember.

Moakley asked if there was a particular way of throwing trash or standards for removing it. Smith said there weren't. Moakley asked him to explain how I could have done my job incorrectly. Smith didn't know. Moakley asked him what that meant. He said that Smith was the boss and he depended on other leaders to give him a proper evaluation of me, and he didn't check out the truth to the stories, and then he destroyed a man's living. Smith said he had done nothing of the kind. Stoneman then jumped in and objected. Moakley said that Smith had been lying through the entire deposition, and Flynn had also been lying. The deposition was a hoax, a joke of the law system. It just proved the town's power and the fact that they had money to waste. Stoneman explained that Smith had a loss of memory because of his medications. Moakley said that was not an excuse. He said I was hanging in the balance as I struggled with the loss of my job, financial problems, and most importantly, health problems. It all stemmed from my former job and Smith's incompetence and lies.

Stoneman told Moakley that his client should not have screwed up his job with the town of Butland. Moakley said we were done with the deposition, and he closed the meeting with the court reporter.

Afterwards, I asked Moakley for his opinion about the deposition. He said the situation looked good for us. Smith and Flynn didn't know anything about their jobs or the everyday operations or even the accusations against me. When I asked Moakley what would happen next, he said we would have to wait for three to four months for a court date with the judge. He said he would keep in touch with you about my workers' compensation case.

CHAPTER 20

FAMILY MEETING AND THE EXPLANATION OF WHITE-COLLAR CRIMES

I HAD EXPERIENCED ANXIETY DURING THE DEPOSITIONS, AND IT increased after the depositions. Moakley had done a good job questioning Smith and Flynn; his questions had brought out many good points in my favor. But I begin to wonder if we had done a good enough job. Had we provided the proper proof that would enable a judge to rule in our favor?

On my way home, I started having a hard time. I had difficulty driving because of the anxiety attacks, which were getting stronger, and the pain. When I eventually got home, my mother asked what had happened at the depositions. I told her I was having an anxiety attack. I needed time to calm down first, and I asked her to call my brothers and my sister to come over so I could explain the situation to all of them at the same time.

When my family were all sitting around the table, I described the depositions and explained how Moakley had asked questions that revealed that I had been dismissed from my job without a proper reason because Robert Smith had not checked the truth of the stories he had heard from the foremen and assistant supervisor. I told them that town attorney Stoneman had objected to a lot of Moakley's questions. The witnesses, Flynn and Smith, had shown that they were lying about their stories. Moakley had accused them of lying, and Stoneman had objected and protected his clients. During the questioning, I believed that Moakley and I were getting to the truth because Flynn and Smith were lying about everything or saying they didn't remember. I believed they had both committed perjury, and the town attorney and the town itself were responsible.

I then said if anyone at the deposition had any doubts about who was at fault, that doubt only reflected that the town was in the wrong. That was brought out by Moakley's questions, which backed up my complaints from the beginning. I told them that I would receive the transcripts, and they could read them. My brother Joseph asked why Moakley had been giving me a hard time with everything up until that time. I said I didn't know why, but we had a long way to go. My brother Anthony reminded me that no one would stand up for me if I didn't stand up for myself. He encouraged me to fight to the bitter end because I was right. I said that we needed to see if Moakley would keep improving his work overtime or if he would let me down. My mother asked if I felt better after seeing that the depositions seemed to have been in my favor. I said yes and no; it all depended on whether the judge would allow the case to go to court where we could prove our side by calling more witnesses and presenting more evidence. I told my family that Moakley hadn't asked more witnesses to come in because I didn't have enough money to cover the expenses. My family didn't like the explanation. My mother told me I had the money. The problem was deciding if we were going to give any more money to Moakley.

I started thinking about how I had researched and found

information about my health issues. Now it was time to look into white-collar crimes, laws that govern medical and legal professionals, and how that information would affect me and my cases.

White-collar crimes have been going on for hundreds of years. White-collar crimes are non-violent crimes that can have a major effect on people, businesses, and governments. Most importantly, they break this country's laws. In my case, the doctors didn't want to write up proper diagnoses and prognoses for my attorney, for me, or for the courts involved in these cases. Doctors who don't keep complete and authentic medical records are breaking laws. There are many other ways that doctors can negligent their patient including prescribing too much or not enough medicine, sexual abuse, and falsifying medical records. False medical records could lead to false legal records in court and much more. My own doctors were guilty of falsifying medical and legal documents, and they could have done other illegal things that I was not aware of. Doctors do not like to cooperate with attorneys and courts, and that is another way they neglect their the responsibilities.

I found that white-collar crimes break many different areas of the law. First, there are criminal acts like bribery, money laundering, fraud, inside trading, embezzlement, and espionage. Then there are also corporate crime, organized transnational crime, and crimes of national interest. Then white-collar crimes run hand in hand with blue-collar crimes, which are mafia-style crimes against businesses, government officials, attorneys, judges, police personnel, and politicians. These two types of crime work together because the blue-collar criminals enforce the crimes of white-collar criminal bosses. This is no different from the government: politicians make the laws, and law enforcement enforce them. All criminals are dishonorable, greedy, and power hungry. The difference between blue-collar crimes and white-collar crimes is that blue-collar crimes involve the physical operation of a crime, and white-collar crime involves the masterminding of the operation. Both are very dangerous, and they work hand in hand with each other. For example, two of our own presidents, John F. Kennedy and Abraham Lincoln, were assassinated. These were white-collar crimes carried out by blue-collar criminals. It is interesting to note that white-collar crimes are more deadly than blue-collar crimes.

White-collar crimes are born of evil and can be deadly. They are the brainstorm of criminals and the downfall of leaders of corruption. This is an age-old problem that stems from people ruthlessly gaining power by destroying their rivals and competitors. These problems have plagued humanity in the past, they are with us today, and they will carry on into our future. I hear these words every day from so many leaders in our world: "I don't care about anything." These leaders set an example for the citizens of our world. This attitude also trickles down to all levels of life, and it is especially sad to hear children say, "I don't care about anything." The worst teachers are the adults of the world. The children start out innocent until they learn about corruption from the adults.

The sad thing about white-collar crimes is that they can happen to anyone, and sometimes they can go undetected for years. One of the reasons is that white-collar crime is not easily identified. And it seems there are no areas that cannot be touched by it. White-collar crimes can go undetected in many ways; they can take place right in front of people, and they don't even notice. Some such crimes include sexual harassment; other kinds of harassing; bribery; and favoritism, which assigns raises and promotions for reasons other than merit. Bribery is a high-level white-collar crime that can be used to protect government officials when they are breaking our laws; for example, suppressing police reports and complaints made to the police; writing letters of complaint to politicians about the conditions of the federal or state or town or city levels. For example, my complaints and letters to government officials were all ignored.

These are only some white-collar crimes that are happening as you are reading these pages. Law enforcement officials don't know how to handle these problems that are running wild throughout the private, business, and government sectors.

Let's not forget the money side white-collar crime; breaking the laws can be quite profitable. Most white-collar criminals are not punished severely when they are found guilty. God forbid top officials should have to pay big money in fines or jail time. If the crime was committed with malicious intention, the fines could be three times bigger than the cost of a lawsuit.

Blue-collar criminals are the enforcers of white-collar crime leaders, but some blue-collar criminals think they are smarter than the white-collar criminals or the police authorities. In reality, blue-collar criminals are the dumbest people around because they are the ones who end up going to jail. The white-collar criminals sit in wealthy homes and live large off the common people who suffer as a result of the blue-collar crimes.

There is so much more to explain about white-collar crimes. There are books full of our laws. There are also true stories in crime books based on real-life information like this one I'm writing for you. I will explain more about white-collar crimes a bit later in this story.

CHAPTER 21

COMPLICATIONS WITH WORKERS' COMPENSATION

A FEW WEEKS AFTER THE DEPOSITION, I CALLED ATTORNEY Moakley and asked about my workers' compensation case. I wanted to know when we would go over the case information. I also asked how long it would take to hear from the US District Court. Moakley said I had to go to his office if I wanted to talk about the workers' compensation case. I met with Moakley with a family member. Before I asked about the workers' compensation case, I asked what was happing with the US District Court. Moakley said that we had to wait for an answer from the judge, who would give us a court date. I said that my retainer with him would not be needed until we went to court, and he agreed. Then I opened the topic of my workers' compensation case, and he asked me what I wanted to know. I looked at him strangely because he should just have answered my question. So, I asked if he followed any particular procedures when working on a workers' compensation case for a client, and if he did, what were they.

Moakley noticed that I was thinking more clearly about the cases now and that I was conducting myself in a more organized and methodical manner. He asked how my health was doing, and I told him that I was trying to manage my anxiety and fibromyalgia, but the pain from fibromyalgia was killing me and my body. I said that the confusion caused by my anxiety was getting better over time. I was thinking more clearly, trying to socialize with people, and trying to occupy myself with productive activities. He said that was all good but we still had a problem because the doctors were not coming forward with the proper paperwork for diagnosis and prognosis. I suggested that we get an independent doctor to evaluate my entire medical case and the court cases. Moakley said that was a good idea, but I would have to pay for the evaluation. He asked if I had the money. I told him I thought that I didn't have to pay for anything that applied to my workers' compensation case, but he said I had to pay for what he called "extras." I told him he should explain to my doctors that he needed the proper medical records to help us prove my workers' compensation case, but he said he had asked them for the medical records, but he hadn't got a response from them. I told him he needed to argue with the doctors or take the problem to the judge and say that the doctors don't want to cooperate with their patient, his attorney, the judge, and the court. Moakley argued with me and said that he couldn't do that in way.

I told him how perfect his questions had been during the depositions with the town. But now he was playing in the opposite direction. I also said he should think of better ways to beat these cases using our laws. I said that he was supposed to have thought about getting an outside doctor who could evaluate this case and prove that my doctors were wrong to withhold my medical information. I had been telling him all along that we did not have a complete set of medical information from my doctors. Therefore, we should bring a case against my doctors for holding back medical information, which is also medical neglect and malpractice. Moakley only said that we could consider that idea later. I told him he was wrong; we could use a lawsuit as leverage against the doctors and force them to cooperate with him as my attorney. The law system works against criminals who don't cooperate with the police, the district attorneys, other attorneys, and the courts. Moakley said I was wrong with all of these ideas.

My temper started to build. I was angry with Moakley because I knew that his answers were wrong. I knew his explanation of the laws with regard to my cases was not right. I had told Moakley that I had talked to other attorneys in the past and I shared some of my conversations with those attorneys. Then Moakley looked at me and lied to my face about the same laws and information that the other attorneys had warned me about with regard to Moakley.

I told him we were going around and around. We needed to look for the laws that would work for the cases. I reminded him that I had been looking for better information that could help both of us win my cases. Moakley only turned his head and ignored my words. I asked him if he could find a doctor who would understand my health conditions, especially fibromyalgia. I said that fibromyalgia was the main problem at that point in the case, but some of my doctors were not acknowledging that diagnosis. Moakley again asked if I had the money to pay an independent doctor to examination my records. I told him he was forcing me to pay for the doctor when it was his job to pay and then take it back as a medical expense at the end of the case. Moakley told me I needed to pay. I said he should have thought about that the first sign that the doctors were not going to cooperate with us. Moakley said that we were doing this now, so it was not a big deal. I said, yes, it was a big deal because we were not prepared for these cases or anything related problems that might come up. I reminded him that the representatives of the town were lying. I told him that, even though I wasn't an attorney, I knew how to be prepared for a case He had lots of training and experience, but he didn't know what to do. Moakley ended that meeting and stated that he would call me when he found a doctor who could do an evaluation. Constantly, Moakley would either leave me hanging or go around and around and provide me with no answers to my questions.

A few weeks later, I received a phone call from Moakley. He told me that that the town was trying to dismiss the workers' compensation case. I asked him if he had filed papers against the town for workers' compensation, and he said he had. I asked them how they could deny the claim, and he said they just could. He wasn't surprised considering they had been doing so much lying. He said that my doctors were making this case harder because they weren't cooperating with the laws. I noticed that Moakley was finally admitting that the doctors were acting illegally. But he still insisted that he couldn't do anything about the doctors on a legal level. I was plagued by Moakley's lies and his misleading information about the laws, and I was plagued by the doctors who wouldn't cooperate. And I was plagued by legal authorities who ignored my reports of criminal behavior. Moakley said we needed to go to Sealand to meet with the town attorney and discuss workers' compensation case. He secured a date for a consultation with a conciliation person. When he passed this information forward to me, I asked if I was going to this meeting. Moakley said I didn't have to, but I wanted to be there, so he said I could go.

Moakley was late for our meeting at the Workers' Compensation Office in Sealand. As usual, he blamed the buses and trains. He asked me if I had seen the town attorney, but I said I hadn't; indeed, I didn't even know who it was. Moakley said he would look for her; I hadn't realized it was a woman. I asked him what her name was, and he said he thought it was Kerry Dunn. When I expressed surprise that he wasn't sure, he walked away from me. Moakley found Kerry

Dunn, and she said that we had to wait to be called. I asked Moakley if he had found out why we were there. When he said no, I asked him if he had talked on the phone with this attorney. Moakley said he had; that's how he knew she was a woman. I asked why he hadn't asked her why we were there.

Moakley was caught in a lie at that point. He said it was only an introductory talk between the attorneys. I asked him if they had talked about the particulars of the case, but he repeated that it was just for introductions. I told him I had a hard time believing that. All attorneys talk about their cases and disclose information about them. That is the law, and he was obligated to disclose his conversation with her to me. That applied to all my cases; there should be no private conversations between attorneys, especially regarding me, his client. Moakley just looked at me with amazement. Then he admitted that I had been doing a lot of homework about the cases and the general laws and medical laws. I agreed that I had done a lot of reading, especially when I didn't understand issues or trust people.

A woman from the office called out my case name, and we were taken to an office to meet with the conciliation official for the Workers' Compensation Office. Those present were Lydia White, conciliation official for the Workers' Compensation Office and the Commonwealth of Rhode Island; Kerry Dunn, attorney for the town of Butland; Allan Moakley, attorney for the plaintiff; and me, the plaintiff.

White stated that this meeting would decide if we would go forward to a workers' compensation judge. Moakley said that he had sent in all the paperwork and medical records, but Dunn interrupted, stating that there was no medical threshold met for requirements by laws. White was bothered by Dunn's interruption and the fact that she was reciting the law. White said that she knew the laws and the rights of the people involved with this case. White said that her job was to determine if the case should go forward to a judge; it was not to determine the case herself. If all the proper paperwork was done, the case would go forward to the judge for a hearing. I agreed that all the appropriate paperwork had been done correctly, and I was eager for the case to go forward to a judge. White then said that Dunn had filed her grievance against Moakley and me. I knew the grievance was full of lies. Attorney Dunn was so upset with this that she asked to speak to Moakley in private. I told Moakley I wanted to hear the conversation, but he said I couldn't because it was a conversation for attorneys only. I asked Moakley if they would tell me about the conversation, but he only avoided the question, and I never heard anything what they had talked about. Like any other person, I tried to listen to the conversation through the door, but I had no luck.

When the conversation was over between the attorneys, I asked Moakley to tell me what they had discussed, but he refused. I told him I knew he wanted me to believe in him, but he was giving me so many reasons *not* to believe in him instead. Moakley said he didn't care what I believed. Moakley said that we had won the decision. Conciliation official White had given us the green light to go in front of a judge. However, he said that I had pissed off Dunn with my answer to one of White's questions. Moakley said I was in a big fight with the town and Attorney Kerry Dunn. I reminded him that he had wanted to go after the workers' compensation case, not me at first, but then I gave in to him. When I asked him if he was going to be able to handle Attorney Dunn and all the town lies and bullshit, he said he was. I asked what the next step was. Did we need to go over the case and prepare for this hearing? He said he'd let me know when he was given a hearing date. When I asked about the independent doctor, he said he was working on it. He had some in mind, but he hadn't decided yet. I reminded him that it had been about two months, and, again, he only walked away from my question.

CHAPTER 22

JUDGE'S DECISION: UNITED STATES DISTRICT COURT DISTRICT OF RHODE ISLAND

On February 17, 2019, I received the news about the federal court hearing. Moakley sent me an email with a decision from a federal Judge Dick Shawburg. I printed out the email and read it. There were reference cases throughout the paperwork, which made the message difficult to understand. When I got to the end, I expected to see a court date. Instead, I read that Judge Dick Shawburg had made a final decision, and it was in favor of the town. Being Italian, I often get really angry and full of hate. I feel as if I want to destroy the world, but I always hold on to my feelings. My mind went on a rampage because I felt betrayed by my attorney, Allan Moakley. The judge had been misled as he made his decision because the depositions taken by the two attorneys, Stoneman and Moakley, were full of lies.

I tried to calm down and get a hold on my senses. This was very difficult because I felt as if I was being taken advantage of in so many ways, and my health problems were also hurting me so much because of all the stress. I had told nothing but the truth to all the people involved with my cases, and nobody cared about me, my health, or the fact that multiple crimes had been committed by those involved in my two cases. The laws of this country and the politicians and judges in charge of these laws had let me down as a citizen and a human being.

I decided to put down the paperwork, buy a case of beer, and drink my night away while listening to the music that helps me with health problems.

The next day, I woke up in pain caused by fibromyalgia. This recurring problem was only getting worse over time. It took me about an hour to get myself together because of the pain, dizziness, headaches, and other problems. When I was ready, I tried to read the court decision again so I could understand and grasp their decision. I had thought that we were looking for a court date, not a decision from the judge. I told myself I needed Moakley to explain what had happened. I called him and asked for an appointment, but he said he could explain over the phone.

Moakley said my case was over, and he would not work on an appeal for me. I asked how it could be over when we didn't even get a chance to go in front of the judge. We had been looking for a court date. What had happened? He told me that the judge decided that he didn't need to waste the court's time with a nuisance case. I asked what that meant. I said that we could bring other witnesses and evidence into court. Moakley said that the judge had made his decisions based only on the depositions. I was so upset. I told Moakley that the depositions were bullshit! I was on a one-way track, and it didn't go anywhere near justice. The case was being discarded. There were very few consequences for the town even though their actions had been responsible for my deteriorated mental health, physical health, and well-being. I said that people who were addicted to drugs or alcohol were treated better at their jobs than someone like me who was a victim of mental abuse and discrimination from their boss.

Moakley said he was out of the case. He said again that he would not represent me in an appeal. I asked why, and I told him that his mistakes were the reason I was in such a mess. I asked if I could see the paperwork he had sent into court, but he said no. The courts had the paperwork, and the courts would not let me see it. He said that I had ten days to write to the judge, and then I had thirty days to appeal. I would have to find an attorney for the appeal. I asked if he would still represent me with the workers' compensation case, and he said he would. I told him he had to pay me back roughly $2,000 of the retainer I had given him. He said he would. He also said he was expecting another date for the workers' compensation case. I asked how long I would have to wait for him to return my money, and he said about two weeks. I asked him about the independent doctor, and he said he'd send me some resumes. I told him we were done, and I hung up the phone.

About a week later, I received a letter from Moakley. I was expecting a check; instead it was a bill for his attendance at the workers' compensation case, the phone call about the judge's decision, and the expenses connected with the depositions that had been taken in late September and early October. I was receiving the bill in late February. Moakley had stolen about $1,600 by submitting these charges. The workers' compensation case should have been free until we settled. The depositions had taken place about five months ago. The only amount that might have been appropriate was the phone call about the judge's decision. I wouldn't have thought that Moakley would charge me for a phone call about an explanation of the decision from the judge. Plus, he had not done his job as an attorney. He had especially made mistakes in the case and had not fought hard enough with the town attorney and the judge to secure a court date for the case.

My mother was in Florida from October to May, and I was home with my sister and her boyfriend. My mother called to ask me how I was doing and my sister was doing. I told her everybody was okay. She asked how the case was going, and I said we all should get together so I could update them all at once. Mother said to gather everyone and then call her. I called Lisa, Joseph, Anthony, and Sarah, and we set a meeting for a Saturday. On that day, we gathered together, called my mother, and I told them about the judge's decision, how Moaklcy had screwed up, and the money that Moakley had stolen from the retainer money. I started with the judge. I told them that Moakley and I had been waiting for a court date, but we got the judge's decision in favor of the town instead. I said that the judge referenced other cases to back up his decision without having a court session. The average citizen wouldn't understand much of the paperwork I had been given. What is a citizen supposed to do with these reference cases? Was I supposed to look up all the reference cases? The average citizen doesn't have access to that information or the knowledge to understand it if he found it. We are an Italian family, so everybody got upset—except Lisa. But she was bothered that the law can let people down without any justice.

Meanwhile, all my family members had opinions, starting with my mother. She said that Moakley had let me down big time, and she suspected that people had been paid off to keep me from fair treatment. Joseph said that the politicians were the real criminals, and they teach our population who follow the lead criminals, who are the politicians. Anthony said the politicians stopped the mafia so that they could take control and be the greedy ones. They were the most powerful because they had all the money. Then they destroyed the small guys and locked them up in jail for the same crimes that they themselves perpetrated every day of their lives. My sister, Sarah, said that the people who come up with the criminal ideas are only the leaders in white-collar crimes, and the crimes are carried out by blue-collar criminals. The criminal activity starts at the top—from the president down to the bums in the streets. Nobody is safe if everybody is on the take or hurting our very system of laws and humanity. I said that the politicians are like the drug dealers. There is never enough money for them, so they take advantage of people and everything they can, including killing them.

I continued to explain to my family how Moakley had sent me an email explaining that the judge had made a decision without a court session. Moakley hadn't even put up an argument to try to get a court session. When I called Moakley, he said that the discrimination case was over, and I would have to find a new attorney for the appeal. When my family heard that, the chaos started. They all argued that Moakley was wrong to leave me in my time of legal need, especially because we hadn't been able to court. They felt he was wrong not to help with my appeal. They felt that he had taken my money and run away with it. Also, they believed that Moakley must have been paid off for intentionally losing the case without a fight. Either that or he had just laid down for them. I said that Moakley had played a game with me, going back and forth, doing right things and wrong things with both cases. We all needed to report what Moakley did wrong so he wouldn't get away with these crimes.

I told them I had been writing multiple letters to the legal authorities but had not heard anything from the recipients. I told them to calm down because I had more to tell them about Moakley. They couldn't believe it when I told them how Moakley had promised to return the $2,000 to me but then sent me an invoice for $1,600. Everybody went crazy at this point, believing that he had stolen my money under false pretenses. I agreed.

I said that government officials and law officials don't want to hear anything to do with these corruption problems within their own system. Again, we talked about my unanswered letters to so many officials at so many levels of government. All my family members agreed that I was the subject of a huge cover-up perpetrated by the town of Butland.

CHAPTER 23

WORKERS' COMPENSATION DAY WITH JUDGE JILL RIP-OFF AND JUDGE JOHN MACK

I RECEIVED A LETTER FROM THE WORKERS' COMPENSATION OFFICE; I was to report to the office for a hearing. Two days later, Attorney Moakley sent an email notifying me about the hearing date. On the day of the hearing, my niece Jane and I showed up for the hearing, and once again, Attorney Moakley was late. When he finally arrived, I asked him what I should expect from the judge. He said he would handle the hearing and told me not to speak to the judge. Jane looked at me as if to say, Are you kidding me about this attorney? Moakley walk into the courtroom to see Judge Jill Rip-Off. Then I saw Attorney Kerry Dunn go into the courtroom. Jane and I went to the courtroom door, and I called out to Attorney Moakley. He asked what I wanted. I told him I wanted to be in the courtroom with all of the people involved with my case. I wanted to hear what everybody was saying. He told me it would be a conversion for only judges and attorneys, not for me. Jane said, "What the hell? This is all about you, not them." Then she said that maybe they were trying to find a way to lose the case against you. I told her I had been thinking the same thing. I couldn't afford to get stressed out. If that happened, I wouldn't be able to deal with conversations or anything at all. So I stood at the open door watching and trying to listen to them. My presence seemed to upset all of them, and I heard the judge say she would take care of the problem.

When the judge said they were ready to begin the hearing, Attorney Moakley called me into the courtroom. The judge started the hearing by making introductions. Present were Judge Jill Rip-Off, a workmen's comp judge, Office of the Commonwealth of Rhode Island; Attorney Alan Moakley, attorney for the plaintiff; Attorney Kerry Dunn, attorney for the town of Butland, and me, Vincent D'Angelo, plaintiff.

The judge asked me to say my name for the record. Then she asked Attorney Moakley to explain why we were there. Moakley said that he was there with his client because his client was suffering from stress-related health issues that had developed as a result of being abused by Superintendent Robert Smith of the town of Butland. He gave the accusations against Robert Smith and the town of Butland as follows: mentally abusing me, discriminating against me, creating a hostile environment at the workplace, threatening my job security, and telling lies about my work performance. He explained how I had originally become ill and how my stress-related symptoms had compounded. After he outlined those symptoms, he told her that, because my nervous system had been compromised by the fibromyalgia, I had also developed phobias. The prognosis was that, over time, my health problems would become more intense, and new health problems could develop as well. He stated that these health problems developed because a bully superintendent abused his power. He also mentioned that Smith had abused other workers in the same manner, and witnesses could be called into court to testify to those allegations. The judge asked if there was anything else. Attorney Moakley said not for the moment.

The judge asked Attorney Kerry Dunn for the town's response to the complaints. Dunn explained that all the information presented on my behalf was untrue. She said that I, the plaintiff, had already lost the discrimination case, and there were no grounds for this case to go forward. Attorney Moakley explained to the judge that there were two different cases; the discrimination case was not relevant to the workers' compensation case we were addressing that day. The judge reminded Dunn that there were two different cases: a civil case and a workers' compensation case. Two different courtrooms; two different sets of laws. She told Dunn that she should know that as a workers' compensation attorney. She asked Dunn if she practiced in any other areas of law, and Dunn said she worked only on workers' compensation cases. The judge told her to stick to the area of law that she knew.

Judge Rip-Off asked Moakley if there was any more information he would like to share with this court. Dunn asked if she could have a minute, and the judge said yes. Dunn recited the words of Federal Judge Dick Shawberg, repeating that I had been a lazy worker and that my work had not been satisfactorily up to the town standards. She said that Robert Smith had spoken to me about these work habits. She said that the town also was in possession of a letter written by my highway foreman complaining about my performance. Judge Rip-Off told Kerry that she was still trying to bring in information and results from a different case. Her information didn't apply to the current case. Judge Rip-Off asked Dunn if she was trying to influence her as the judge. Dunn said she wasn't. I stood up to say something to the judge about Dunn's statement, but the judge told me that I needed to be quiet and just sit there. Jane was sitting in the back of the courtroom and was astonished when she heard what the judge said to me. Jane knew I just wanted to explain that Dunn was lying to the court.

Judge Rip-Off said she had decided how we would move forward. We would take the case to mediation with a judge to see if we could all agree to satisfactory solution. The judge had noticed that I wanted to say something, so she asked if I wanted to speak. I told her that I wanted this to go to a trial so we could present witnesses and evidence. The judge said that we would first have to try mediation. If that didn't work, we could have a hearing. She said that, as a judge, she was strongly suggesting that we accept the mediation appointment where we would discuss money and a possible settlement. If we decided not to accept, there was a chance that she might not allow the case to go forward. Judge Rip-Off said that I wouldn't like the answer she would give me that day if I disagreed. Then she said that she would hold off on making a decision based on what had gone on that day. Then she would wait until she had the mediation results.

After the hearing, Moakley spoke to the judge. Later, he told me that the judge wasn't happy about Dunn trying to influence her with information from the other case. I asked Moakley what the judge meant by telling me to take the mediation date. Moakley said that the judge would have denied my case if all she had to go on was that day's hearing. Moakley said we had done okay that day. He said he had other clients to see that day, so we parted company.

As Jane and I walked to the car, she asked how I felt. I told her I had terrible pains throughout my body. Jane asks if I could drive. I told her I would try, but my anxiety was starting to build up, pushing the pain throughout my body. I told Jane to watch my driving, and if I needed to pull over, I would. When we finally made it home, Jane said the judge had been an asshole about the entire case and had then pushed me to go to mediation so the case would be dragged out even longer. I agreed.

About two weeks later, I received two letters from the Workers' Compensation Office. The first provided a mediation date in three months. The second letter said Judge Rip-Off had denied compensation based on the complaints we presented on the day of the hearing. The judge had lied about waiting for the mediation date before making her decision. The judge had made her decision before we started the hearing that day. I wondered why she had encouraged me to agree to mediation that was now not relevant.

I called Jane and asked her if she had heard the judge say she would hold off on her decision until the mediation had taken place. Jane said she had. I told her that the judge had denied my claim on the day of the hearing. I said she had actually made her decision even before the hearing started. Jane asked what that meant; I said we needed to appeal the case immediately.

Next, I called Moakley and asked him if he had received any paperwork from the Workers' Compensation Office. He said he hadn't. I said I had, and the judge had denied the case. Moakley said we would appeal the decision. He also said that we had the mediation date, and hopefully, we would settle then.

Three months later, we went back to Sealand where it cost me another $40 to park, and I had no income. My mother and my daughter were with me. Once again, Moakley was late, and when he did show up, I asked him what would happen that day.

Moakley said that we would see the mediation judge and try to come to a settlement that day. I was on edge because I was worried about the mediation process. I had never been involved with any kind of mediation, so I didn't know what to expect.

Judge John Mack would handle the mediation. He would separate the two sides of the case and have them sit in two separate rooms. Then he would go back and forth between rooms with a settlement amount each time. I asked Judge Mack why he was separating us. I had thought we would be in the same room. He said we would be separated because the town representatives would be on the phone talking to their attorney, but I could speak to my attorney in person without any pressure. We started at about 9:30 in the morning, and we were told it should take about three hours to reach a settlement.

The judge started by asking Moakley and me to provide a starting number. I told him that, according to my own research, I would be suffering with my health problems for the rest of my life. I said I was going to start at $500,000. Judge Mack said that my information about my future health was not a factor with that settlement, but he would give the other side the amount.

Moakley said that I would never get that number; I should have started lower. I said, "Are you kidding me? Don't any of my health problems come into play with that settlement?" Moakley said they didn't. So I asked him why were we wasting time over nothing if he wasn't going to include my health problems. I asked what he was basing a money amount on. He said that my case was a nuisance case at that point. I told him he was the one who had pushed for a workers' compensation case, not me.

At that moment, the judge returned with a counteroffer of $20,000. I said, "You are kidding me! This is just a waste of my time!" I told them that I knew they were all just prolonging the proceedings and making them more difficult so that I would settle for a lot less. And saying that my health didn't matter at this point was bullshit.

The judge told me to calm down. He would try to get me a settlement I could be comfortable with. He said he assumed I didn't like the $20,000 offer, and I said I didn't. I said I would lower my request to $100,000. He said that sounded like a more reasonable number. The judge left the room to talk to the town attorney, and I told Moakley that the mediations procedures sucked! I told him that we knew what was happening in the other room. The judge had been sitting down and having a regular conversation with us, and I assumed he was doing the same over there in the other room. He was wasting time. Moakley said he didn't know, but he assumed that, if the judge was talking with us, he was probably doing the same with the opposition.

Judge Mack returned with an offer of $35,000. I said that wasn't enough. There was something wrong with these offers and procedures. I said that a federal judge had denied me my day in court, and I had lost my case. Now I was struggling over a workers' compensation settlement. I would have to deal with all of my health problems for the rest of my life, and I was being offered only $35,000! Judge Mack asked how all that had happened.

Moakley explained that we had been waiting for a court date, but the federal judge had decided to base his decision only on the depositions. Judge Mack said that he had never heard of a judge dismissing a case in such a way. Moakley said he hoped we could come to an answer that day on the workers' compensation case because he would be on vacation for two weeks. Judge Mack asked if I accepted the offer of $35,000, and I said I didn't. I wanted $50,000. If they didn't agree, we would have to go back to the case judge. Judge Mack went back to the town representatives. After a while, he returned and said that they had agreed to pay $50,000.

Attorney Kerry Dunn walked by the door and said she had to go to her next appointment. Moakley said he had to leave, but I knew it was because of his vacation, and Judge John Mack was also getting ready to leave. I asked where Dunn was going. I thought we had to sign papers to finalize the agreement. The judge started to speak, but Moakley interrupted him and said that, when he got back from his vacation, we would sign the papers, and the ordeal for me would be all over. I said I hoped he was right because every time I had to explain these cases and health problems, my body went through anxiety and pain because of my fibromyalgia, and that was not good for my health. It was as if I was repeatedly reliving my problems. I could not escape them. Moakley said it would be all over when he came back. Moakley confirmed to my mother and daughter that we had reached a settlement in the amount of $50,000.

On our way home after the workers' compensation mediation, I explained what had happened to my mother and daughter. I told them how they had separated us and how I had asked at first for $500,000, which was denied. Then the second amount of $100,000 was denied. Then I asked for $50,000, and the town agreed. I explained how the judge had carried out a regular conversation with us as if he hadn't been there to do a mediation job. I said I would like to know what was going on between the town representatives and the judge. Meanwhile, I explained how Moakley and I got into issues while we waited for the judge to return.

My mother and daughter were glad it would be all over when Moakley returned from his vacation. I said that had bothered me. Moakley was going on vacation, and Attorney Kerry Dunn had run out after we came to an agreement. Even the judge left in a hurry. Moakley had promised we would sign the papers when he got back from vacation. I had asked Moakley if the town could back out of the agreement; he assured me it would be all over when he got back. My mother and daughter told me not to worry; I said we would see in two weeks when the check was in my hands.

Two weeks later, I called Moakley and asked if he had the papers to sign for the settlement we had agreed on with the town. Moakley said he had bad news for me—the town had withdrawn the agreement. I said, "What! Are you kidding me, Allan?" He said he wasn't. We would have to appeal the judge's decision, and now we had to go to court to argue the case. I asked Moakley why couldn't the mediation judge confirm that we had an agreement. That would prove that the town representatives and their attorney had been lying about the entire case, and that information might have some bearing on the other case as well. Moakley said no. The other case was over. I told him that, if new information came up, they would have to reopen the discrimination case. Moakley said that I was mistaken. He would get in touch with me when he received a date for the case.

When I got off the phone with Moakley, I explained to my mother that the town had withdrawn the settlement. Then I said that the situation had been orchestrated; it had all been a big, showy game. My mother agreed.

CHAPTER 24

MEETING FRIENDS FROM WORK
AT A FAMILY FUNCTION

In the summer of 2018, my family and I were invited to a family memorial for my Uncle Brian, who had passed away. At this memorial, I happened to meet up with friends from work and friends of my family who lived in Butland. My Aunt Jerry, the wife of Uncle Brian, was there with their five children. My cousins lived in Butland, Rhode Island. They were very well known in Butland and many other towns in the area, just as I was. I had lived in Butland at one time. I had worked run my own construction business there and worked for other companies. I also used to hang out and play in Butland when I was growing up. I was the younger cousin, always tagging along with my older cousins and their friends, hanging out with them and having fun. When I got older, I rented an apartment in Butland behind the old Roxie's store and worked for a cabinet company building countertops for cabinets. Later, when I started my business, I worked on all types of carpentry jobs. I was also a member of the Sons of Italy. I worked and hung out with many friends in the town of Butland. In those days, times were good. I was making money, socializing with good friends, and living in my apartment.

My family and I went to the memorial where I also was surprised to meet up with many friends from the DPW office: Richie, Moe, highway foremen Scott, and Ryan. I also met other friends from Butland. My cousins' friends also knew all about my problems with the Butland officials.

We all greeted each other and started to talk about the old days. Some of the guys asked how my business was doing. They asked if I was still plowing for Butland. I told them I was not working for myself anymore. I said I had had a job with the DPW office in Butland, but I lost my employment because of Robert Smith. Then they started asking me about what had happened with the DPW job. I told them that Smith had started harassing me, discriminating against me, bullying me, and threatening my job. All my friends said they had heard bad stories about Smith; they all said I wasn't the first one to be screwed by him. They said he looked for people he could control by holding situations over their heads with threats and creating problems, especially when they didn't cooperate with his rules, which were totally apart from the town's rules.

I told him that had happened to me because he wanted me to be a stoolie and spy on the men I worked with. Smith figured I was a new employee, and it would be easy to push me around, but I wasn't the kind of a person to rat on my friends or coworkers. I had learned early in life that workers and bosses had different goals with respect to work conditions. Workers needed to trust their fellow workers because, someday, one of those workers could save their lives. Bosses, however, don't work with the workers. They just sit in their offices barking orders.

When I was working with the sixty men from the DPW office, many of them had warned me that I should be careful around Smith because he could hurt me and jeopardize my job. Some of the residents of Butland stopped me as I was plowing and complained about Smith. It's amazing that nobody ever instigated some type of investigation into Smith or the town hall. Smith created all kinds of problems for the workers and residents. He would start problems by intentionally setting workers against each other. Then he would do nothing to solve the problems that resulted. He also would use workers against other workers personally. All my friends said that Smith was notorious for the head games he played on the workers. After we talked for a while about Smith, my friend Scott finally made the most damaging statement about Smith. First, he told us about Smith's suspension and how J. B. had taken on the job as acting superintendent for about two years. Scott said that Smith had control over the association union within the DPW office. This wasn't a traditional union. A traditional union would be a totally separate entity and not part of the DPW office, and Smith would not be a member. At the DPW office, Smith controlled the association union officials and five members from the office. These men were also the same workers that Smith controlled within the DPW office.

Scott exploded with information about the DPW office. He said that the leaders of the DPW office and town hall officials were corrupt. Scott explained all the dirty deeds that had been happening at the DPW office, just as I had experienced when I was working there back in 2014. Scott said that Smith had been pushed into retirement in 2015 because of his dirty deeds and *my* lawsuits! He wasn't a threat to the workers anymore. Now the workers were talking about all the problems that still existed because of Smith's illegal behavior, including my own problems, which had begun in 2014.

Scott told me, in front of eight workers, that they had all been trying to give me information about all the problems within the DPW office because they knew that Smith had wrongfully dismissed me from my job. The reason was that Smith had other plans for me, as he did for many other new workers who came in over time. Smith discriminated against many of the workers in some way. Scott said that Smith couldn't just keep saying that the workers were not fitting in or that their work was inferior. People would catch on if he continued to use the same complaints. So Smith had begun to be creative in dismissing workers. He wouldn't reveal too much information about the illegal steps he was taking against them. He would cover up situations until someone like me brought a lawsuit against him and the town.

The other side of the problem was that the officials in the town hall had protected Smith for as long as they could. Finally, he had been suspended when other problems he had created were exposed. Scott said that some eyebrows within the town hall had been raised when Smith fired me. And that eventually led to Smith's forced retirement. Scott said that Smith was due to retire in 2017, but instead he retired in 2015, about a year after I lost my job. This decision came down from the town hall office because of the two lawsuits I had set against the town and Smith. My actions had pushed the selectmen and other officials to face the problem. They'd had enough of Smith creating problems for the town. Scott said that, before I came into the job, Smith and two other DPW office workers had received a very high raise. Smith's was something like 80 percent. Scott said that I had been Smith's fall guy. But Smith was the fall guy after the town officials realized what Smith had done to me.

Scott apologized for everything that had happened. He told me that Smith had made him write a letter about me. Smith made him lie in the letter and say that my work habits were below standard. Smith had the power to terminate men or make their jobs very difficult. Scott defended them by saying they all had families, but I reminded him that I also had a family. I told him I had lost my health, and that was a life-long condition. I would be in pain every day. Eventually

I might have to use a wheelchair. There was so much that doctors didn't know about the future of my health conditions.

Meanwhile, our friends had heard everything that Scott had said. Then he said he had more information from the town. I told him I was having a hard time taking in everything that he was saying. I told him that, because I had so many health problems, I wanted to record all his information so I could present it to the proper authorities. I also wanted the other guys to verify Scott's stories. One of the guys said that many people had predicted that Smith would hurt me and my job. Smith had done the same to many other employees in the past, and he would do it to others in the future. The town had protected Smith by retiring him so that he could preserve his pension. I told them that I knew they didn't know about how ill and hurt I had become as a result of Smith's actions. But now that they knew about my health problems, didn't they want to help me set the record straight? Scott said I didn't understand the severity of the problems that the town could cause for their families. I said that was why we should stand together and fight this ugly conspiracy between the town and Smith. I told them about my fight with my doctors and my letters to all the government authorities. I said that, together, we could show the town, state, and country that they were not untouchable. They were just as responsible for their white-collar crimes as any other criminal. I also told my friends that, from the start of my employment, Smith had wanted me to spy on them and rat them out, but I chose not to do that. I would not be his stoolie. Finally, I asked them, if town officials had that much power, then what sort of power do the state and federal officials have? I said that might explain why I hadn't heard anything from the officials I'd written my letters to.

After the memorial function for my uncle came to an end that night, I knew much more about what had happened with Smith and the town, especially information related to my employment and termination. So many people were involved in a conspiracy and a cover-up. The next day, I invited my family to come to our house so could pass along all the information I had found out about Butland at the function. My mother invited everyone for dinner, and as we ate our meal, I explained what my friends had said. I reminded my family about my association with Butland over the years when I had lived there and worked there. I was acquainted with customers, friends, family members, and members of Sons of Italy in Butland. I said that a I had lived a big part of my life in Butland a well as other nearby towns. During the memorial function for Uncle Arthur, my friends from the DPW office had talked with me. During our conversations, they realized that they had allowed Smith and the town hall officials to hurt and then destroy a man's life. But the threat to their jobs, and therefore the well-being of their families, weighed heavily on their minds. Each of them, after hearing my story, realized that they had made a mistake allowing Smith and the town government to do so much damage to so many people including me. Then Scott had exposed other wrongdoings of Smith and town hall officials.. If the pension board found out that Smith had extended criminal influence over his job, they would cancel his pension. I had been set up for failure with the town because of Smith and his corrupt ways.

Everyone in my family began to express their frustration, and I knew that their observations and enthusiasm could cause significant legal problems for us all. I told them that I felt the same way they felt, but we couldn't act that way. It was illegal. I said that there are other ways of handling illegal actions taken by Smith and the town officials. The town officials had controlled the crimes (white-collar crimes leaders) and Smith had carried them out (blue-collar crimes and muscle), so we had to continue to write letters until someone finally answered. Joseph asked if my friends would come forward with their information. I told him they wouldn't. The threat that the town held over them was too serious. There would be consequences for their families if they lost their jobs. I explained that I had asked if I could record them as they gave me their accurate information, but they had refused. I told my family that I would find a way to handle these problems on a legal level. I would never stoop to criminal tactics the way Smith and the town officials had. I said that a trail of paperwork was the worst thing in the world for criminals because it could be used against the town and Smith. The main problem was going to be getting the law officials to read the letters and listen to the public and my complaints about this situation. I said that a significant unknown rule of the government was to pit the people against each other at all times. Now we had to try to reverse that situation and make them listen to us. If we could prove that the beginning of the story was a big lie, then we could expose that everything after that was a giant conspiracy that included the attorneys, doctors, judges, and anyone I had written letters to. It was like a domino effect!

CHAPTER 25

GOVERNMENT, LAWS, AND THE CDC

THE BOOK OF GENESIS IN THE BIBLE TELLS US THAT GOD CREATED a world—heaven and earth—within six days. Then God created man and woman on the earth and gave them a set of rules. As time passed, God set forth a new set of laws for the world to obey and follow. They were called the Ten Commandments:

1. You shall have no other gods before me.
2. You shall make no idols.
3. You shall not take the name of the Lord your God in vain.
4. You shall keep the sabbath day holy.
5. You shall honor your father and your mother.
6. You shall not murder.
7. You shall not commit adultery.
8. You shall not steal.
9. You shall not bear false witness against your neighbor.
10. You shall not covet.

From the beginning of time, law and order were always necessary for the universe, our planet, and the people of the land. As society started to grow and new nations were born, the need for laws and rules grew more prominent. The laws of the land will continue to grow over time as our civilization grows. The preservation of law and order will be a challenge over time and through the generations. The laws of God were made to establish equality between men and women throughout the land over a long time. However, God's laws and humanity's laws have been broken repeatedly over the ages. People kept breaking the laws in so many new ways that those in power had to change the laws just as fast to keep up with the criminals.

Over the years, citizens of the world adapted to multiple changes in the law. Before technology, crimes were carried out with spears, knives, swords, bows and arrows. Over time, humans developed devious weapons and strategic plans. And our government has developed laws that have pitted people against each other. Greed inspired the building of empires—the Egyptians, the Romans, and the Ottomans. Finally, there was the British Empire. Slavery was a result of nations and countries conquering other countries in wars that, in their time, were more significant than anyone could imagine in today's world. History is full of brutal bloodshed. When gun powder was invented, an entirely new technology was born. Shortly after that, the steam engine changed the world. By the 1900s, combustible engines were invented along with many more innovations like electricity and gas for the combustible engines. From the 1900s forward, technology increased at an unbelievable rate, and so did the rate of crime and the number criminals who perpetrated them. The immigrants who came to America brought their criminal ways with them, joining with the criminals who were already here. The politicians and leaders became greedy as their wealth and controlling power increased.

Today's world is run by computers, and I believe they are more dangerous than any weapon manufactured in the past. Today's computers control the weapons of destruction that could completely destroy the planet. They also control so many things we rely on every day: phones, vehicles, appliances, utility systems, and so forth. Computers also create trails of information—like old fashioned paper trails—that will never be erased, unlike actual paper that is easy to destroy in many ways. Permanent digital records follow us and our families and exist long after we are gone. This digital record, unfortunately, contains the lies that people tell. Once the lies are computerized, no one can dispute them. But they can be erased, and once the information is gone, the damage it cause is gone as well. The criminals in the age of technology know how these things work, so they do their dirty deeds in the shadows without any public knowledge. Honest people who uphold this country's laws don't see their activities.

The United States of America is being run by government officials and leaders who are following in the footsteps of a long line of criminals that has been here since our continent was discovered so many years ago. The government also allows criminal action from outside forces who have, for generations, hurt the people of the world. This was the beginning of white-collar crime, and it was fueled by power and greed. The powerful stole the land and the wealth of the people. The lies perpetrated by our government have quashed the American dream and damaged the people, past and present.

The laws reflect and uphold our government, which is made up of the people who make the laws. The innocent or intentional mistakes made at the beginning of any investigation are despicable. They have compromised the most basic citizens' rights that were intended to be protected by the laws in this country. In my case, I asked for an investigation by all the proper governmental authorities, the media, and coworker friends. The government and media ignored me. My friends told me that their jobs would be on the line if they cooperated; they would most likely be fired. No man, woman, or child should ever be afraid of reporting any crime or criminals. I have also reported to my doctors and challenged them with information published by the CDC and other authoritative institutions, but I have had no results.

I have spent a lot of time researching the law and medical information on the Internet. I thought I was gaining overall knowledge about following the laws myself and doing the right thing so that I would be successful in my legal cases. But then, medical and legal professionals told me not to follow the information I had found online. I found that advice amusing. Computers were invented for many reasons, but they do provide access to the Internet where everyone can learn about so many topics. But when I tried to use this sort of information to prove my point on a subject, I was told I could not use the information I had learned. In today's world, computers are used by all top officials—senators and congressmen, governors, attorney generals, attorneys, judges, doctors, and police personnel.

Anyone can learn some history by searching the Internet. The crimes and other "games" that our leaders and officials have been involved in over time and throughout our history are documented. When a man stands alone with his complaints about the legal and medical systems, people should get involved because, one day, they too could be involved in a similar losing battle with government officials, lawyers, and doctors. Never leave a person behind for any reason.

Remember the true words and the true thoughts behind our Constitution of the United States. Today, the Constitution has little meaning in our country—not to government leaders, or even the general public. To them, it's just a piece of parchment covered in words that have no meaning to our government or the people. Our government uses the Constitution for convenience, just as it uses the laws. Members of our government can't even get along and work for the good of the people, yet they expect the citizens to get along with each other. We learn from our government—if they don't follow the laws they made for the ordinary, law-abiding citizens, why should they expect the people to follow the laws? Remember that shit rolls downhill, and it rolls down from our president all the way to the homeless people in our streets. Our government isn't doing its job correctly in any way, and that includes all official offices.

We, the people of America, should take back our government and fire everyone who currently holds a powerful government job. Then we should hire new people who will uphold the laws of this country. We should put a ceiling on their pay, limit their terms in office, and hold them responsible for every action they take while they are in office, and even after they leave office. This done, our taxes could be used to better the lives of all citizens. Eventually, we could cut back the taxes. Overall, we, the people, are just slaves forced to pay the taxes to our US Government while our government continues to move in the wrong direction, hurting American citizens and societies worldwide. The government gets away with breaking the law. Remember that only a few things don't discriminate in life; one is death. Death comes to everyone no matter his or her race, religion, financial status, level of health, or any other category we could think of. Another thing that doesn't discriminate in life is taxes. Either we pay, or we go to jail.

When a citizen reports any criminal complaint to the proper government authorities, that complaint should be taken seriously and not pushed off or ignored. Unfortunately, this didn't happen with my cases, and I bet I am not alone. The professionals involved with my cases—doctors, attorneys, and judges—never took the time to hear what I had to say. For example, doctors have a significant influence in legal cases because they provide medical information that attorneys and judges need to ensure just results. Remember, the little people make up the majority of the population, and they need protection from those who commit criminal offenses, including white-collar crimes, that infest our country and world. There are a lot of white-collar crimes that are not even investigated, if they are reported at all, because the powerful people behind them, and the powerful people in positions of authority don't even acknowledge them. This is one of the reasons it is sometimes illegal to make audio recordings of conversations. But this is one of the only ways to expose white-collar criminals, especially when their crimes have to do with high officials or rich people taking advantage of others. It's okay for legal authorities to listen in on conversations among members of the mafia or drug dealers; otherwise, forget about it. "Regular" people can't record government officials to prove they are involved in crimes. Real white-collar crimes start in the offices of government officials and businesspeople. This is how the controversy starts with our government and leaders and secret societies that control our world. The current laws, many of which were made long ago, don't fit the problems of today's world. The rich and powerful can manipulate these laws to commit white-collar crimes to gain more power and wealth. Our government leaders and the laws they uphold should set an excellent example that protect people's rights and safety. Our country is the product of a history that was wrong from the beginning. The laws of the land and people's rights have been violated time and time again. It's no wonder more blue-collar crimes are committed every day. Criminals compete against each other for survival and personal gain.

The reality is that our government system, politicians, laws, secret societies, law enforcement personnel on all levels, banks, corporations, and other leaders worldwide are the problems of our world. Through their cooperation, criminals get away with white-collar crimes. Politicians and business leaders are the planners of crimes in our world. And they allow blue-collar crimes to be carried out. The perpetrators need muscle to enforce dirty deeds and tactics. They want regular people to do as the leaders want, in their favor. Examples are two presidents. John F. Kennedy and Abraham Lincoln were murdered by our government leaders who hired assassins to carry out the blue-collar crime of murder. There are so many criminal elements right in front of our own eyes every day, and we don't even think about them or act in any way to expose them. We, the people, have the power to fire the leaders and put them behind bars for the crimes they commit.

In 2016, President Trump elected as the forty-fifth president of the United States. He treated his presidency as a business, not as a platform for personal gain and power the way other politicians do. As a result, the country started to prosper. Our economy and finances improved, and our borders were secure. The amount of drugs that crossed the borders was nearly reduced to nothing as was the number of illegal immigrants who came into our country. President Trump had to do battle with Capitol Hill and government officials who attacked every step he took. This was a despicable way for government leaders to behave. Think of government officials as the mothers and fathers of our country and the citizens as their children. But when the proper father (President Trump) came into the office, the secondary mothers and fathers had so many complaints that they had no standing when the father (President Trump) spoke. When the end of every day comes, our government is carrying on with secrets, breaking the laws that the government invented, and outright lying to the people who depend on that government.

When will true Americans citizens take a stand against our government? When are the citizens of America going to say they've had enough with our government? When will they fire all the corrupt people from their offices? So many past empires fell because the people got tired of the lies and betrayal of their governments, so they instituted uprisings.

Will history repeat itself in our present time? President Joe Biden is the new puppet whose strings are being pulled by those who hold the real power in our government. President Biden has been criticized by citizens and even by members of multiple government branches. There should be an age cutoff for any government position. Perhaps they should all retire at seventy years old. In all the years that have passed, we have never had a good president to run our country that everybody agreed with, and we never will.

CHAPTER 26

DR. LORI ICEBERG AND
MY INTERNET RESEARCH

I HAD TAKEN THE TIME TO TRY TO EXPLAIN TO MY PRIMARY CARE doctor, Dr. Lori Iceberg, the seriousness of my cases and the fact that it was essential to their outcome that my medical records and information were submitted to be used in court as evidence. I had an appointment coming up with Dr. Iceberg. This time I planned to take to her the information I had gained from my Internet research as I had done with Dr. Orlando.

Meanwhile, my family members and I didn't understand why my doctors weren't cooperating by sending my records to my attorney, who had requested them. My family members believed that the doctors were not doing their jobs correctly or professionally. Maybe there was an alternative reason for their lack of cooperation with my attorney or me. My family members and I started thinking that it was possible that officials from the town of Butland had bribed the doctors. Or maybe some similar games were being played. Any type of a bribe from the town could totally sabotage my cases. So were the doctors being bribed, were they playing games, or were they just incompetent?

I thought about why a doctor wouldn't back up a patient who was suffering from mental and physical disabilities. I looked over the medical records that I had from my doctors, and I saw a lot of information about my illnesses. But I noticed that no doctors had included post-traumatic stress disorder (PTSD) in my records. The doctors had documented all the other conditions related to PTSD along with other health conditions. PTSD is a mental disability. Symptoms include intrusive memories, avoidance, negative changes in thinking and mood, changes in physical and emotional reactions, anxiety, and depression. All my health problems are related to stressful experiences—IBS, fibromyalgia, tension headaches, and nervous system problems. Then I experienced secondary problems of pain in my joints and muscles among other problems.

I found the following information about PTSD on the Mayo Clinic website (https://www.mayoclinic.org/diseases-conditions/post-traumatic-stress-disorder/symptoms-causes/syc-20355967).   The headlines and the list are taken directly from the site. The examples are my own words.

Intrusive memories

1. Recurrent, unwanted distressing memories of the traumatic event.
2. Example: boss bullying, harassing on the job, racial discrimination on the job, verbally abuse.
3. Reliving the traumatic event as if it were happening again (flashbacks).

Example: I relived my experiences every time I had to explain them to doctors, therapists, attorneys, and judges. It was especially troubling when nobody believed me.

4. Upsetting dreams or nightmares about the traumatic event.
5. Severe emotional distress or physical reactions to something that reminds you of the traumatic event.

Example: I experienced stress every time I thought of how my boss treated me when I was working for the town.

Avoidance

1. Trying to avoid thinking or talking about the traumatic event.

Example: I often locked myself in my room, and I spent a lot of time sleeping.

2. Avoid places, activities, or people that remind you of the traumatic event.

Example: I didn't want to do anything that reminded me of my job experiences, my termination, or my subsequent legal battles.

Negative changes in thinking and mood

1. Negative thoughts about yourself, other people, or the world.
2. Hopelessness about the future.
3. Memory problems include not remembering important aspects of the traumatic event.
4. Difficulty maintaining close relationships.

5. Feeling detached from family and friends.
6. Lack of interest in activities you once enjoyed.
7. Difficulty experiencing positive emotions.
8. Feeling emotionally numb.

Changes in physical and emotional reactions

1. Being easily startled or frightened.
2. Always being on guard for danger.
3. Self-destructive behavior, such as drinking too much or driving too fast.
4. Trouble sleeping.
5. Trouble concentrating.
6. Irritability, angry outbursts, or aggressive behavior.
7. Overwhelming guilt or shame.

This was one of many pieces of information that I found as I researched medical and legal issues. I was surprised that my medical records contained nothing about PTSD. I couldn't believe that my doctors, psychiatrist, and therapy counselor had not seen these symptoms along with all the other stress-related problems. But, these doctors weren't writing my records so that my attorneys could use them to win my court cases. The scary thing to me was that these professional doctors had gone through at least eight years of schooling before they could practice, and yet they hadn't seen any of the symptoms of PTSD. I know I am not a qualified doctor or an attorney, but I'm smarter than my doctors, attorneys, judges, and everyone else involved with my cases. All I had to do was look up all the information on Internet websites. The professionals had wasted eight years of study, and I needed only a few hours to research my information. I also submitted to doctors medical evaluations from independent doctors, but my doctors said that I had made up the evaluations. They didn't believe the medical documents that were given to the judges in support of these cases. My medical records were being ignored by both medical and legal professionals simultaneously. The fact that my entire set of medical records was being ignored meant that the small amount of medical information that the attorneys and judges had consisted of false and incomplete information. This led to false legal documents and judgments.

The day came for my appointment with Dr. Iceberg. After the nurse recorded my vital signs and asked me about my medications, I met with Dr. Iceberg. When she asked me how my symptoms were doing, I told her that my pains were getting worse every year. The weather had begun to affect my pains. I was having more frequent headaches. My joints were killing me, my muscles were starting to hurt, and I had been experiencing chest pains. I also had a new problem: my spine had begun to hurt throughout the day and night. All of the pains kept me from falling asleep or staying asleep when I finally did go to sleep. I also had been having dreams that made no sense. As I explained my symptoms, Dr. Iceberg typed the information into her computer. She asked if I was taking my prescriptions, and I said I was taking them when I needed to. She asked why I wasn't taking them the way she had prescribed. I told her I was sensitive to the medicine, and I didn't know why. I explained that the pain medicine and the muscle relaxer both knocked me out for two days. If I took the medications the way she prescribed. I would never see the world again because I'd sleep my life away. When I asked her if she had received the X-rays from Dr. Orlando, she said no. I told her she should look at them because they explained some of my pain. Dr. Iceberg told me to tell her what Dr. Orlando had said to me. I told her I had bone spurs and bone loss in my neck. I had a bulging disk in the middle of the back and another one in my lower back along with arthritis. I was also suffering from hip pain because the joints were wearing down.

Dr. Iceberg said that she couldn't find the X-rays. I asked her why my symptoms were getting worse even though I was not working. I asked if it was because of my fibromyalgia. Then I asked her what she was going to do for me. Dr. Iceberg said that she didn't have an answer for me. She believed I was faking my symptoms and I should go back to work. That set off a switch in my mind. I told her she was a hundred percent wrong! I said we should start with the X-rays she didn't want to believe and Dr. Orlando's diagnoses she didn't want to believe. Then we'd move on to the independent doctors from the town and the court, and my personal independent doctor, all of whom she didn't believe. "Why?" I asked her. "What is your problem?"

Dr. Iceberg was quiet. Then I began to tell her about my Internet medical research. She interrupted me and said that no Internet website had any influence in her office. I explained that the CDC should be recognized in her office because it was a government-run agency staffed by top medical professionals. I told her about the information I had found about stress-related problems that applied to me. I asked her why she hadn't diagnosed me with PTSD. Why hadn't the psychiatrist and the therapist recognized that I had PTSD? Once again, Dr. Iceberg was quiet. I told her that, according to everything I had read, I had all the signs of PTSD, but she hadn't included that in my records. I told her she had doctors' report and X-rays, but she was ignoring the facts. I told her she was violating my rights, personal and health, which meant that she was also violating our country's laws. I told her she was withholding medical information from the courts, which is punishable under federal and state laws. Her lack of attention and cooperation could affect all the medical information and doctors involved in my two cases. It's almost impossible to prove the existence of medical conditions in a courtroom without the proper documents from medical professionals.

I told Dr. Iceberg that she was a doctor who knew about mental health problems, but she was not including information about my mental health and my stress-related problems in my records. I asked her why she couldn't be more like the compassionate doctors portrayed in television commercials who helped people with health problems, especially mental stress and mental health problems. There are hotlines for all types of health issues. Specialists try to help people who call. And there she was, in person, unwilling to even see the facts in the records—records of other doctors, and from her patient directly. I told her I was her patient and a person. She had been disregarding my explanation of what had happened to me and how those experiences had negatively affected my health.

It's a well-known fact that people can get stressed out just from doing their jobs, but a boss who bullies, harasses, and discriminates can compound that stress, especially if he goes around bragging about how he gives a hard time to people intentionally on the job. I had written to doctors, attorneys, judges, and government officials to complain about criminal actions against me, and still I had received no results. My life was not improving. I asked her how she could think that all of this would not take a toll on any person. And how could she think it would not take a toll on a person with multiple stress disorders. Dr. Iceberg told me that, if I didn't like her services, I should find another doctor. I told her that, if I tried to find a new doctor or attorney, the town attorney would be able to say that I was shopping around professionals who would be willing to further my cause, and that would only make me look bad in front of the judge. So, I felt it was best to continue working with the professionals I was already working with. Plus, I didn't think another doctor would want to go through her records and sort out the facts after she had messed up everything. I told her she hadn't even been able to help me get Supplemental Security Income (SSI) benefits. I told her that, when my cases were over, I would instigate an investigation into all the professionals I had worked with. Medical, legal, and court records along with witnesses would prove that professionals had taken advantage of me, a person with mental and physical health issues and legal problems.

CHAPTER 27

ATTORNEY MOAKLEY AND THE WORKERS' COMPENSATION OFFICE

Attorney Moakley and the Workers' Compensation Office both sent me notices about a hearing at the Sealand Workers' Compensation Office. I set up a meeting with Attorney Moakley so that we could talk about this case. He emailed me, telling me to go to his office on Monday at 10:00 in the morning, and he added that the town had given me another offer.

On Monday, I went to Moakley's office with my mother. First, I asked about the mediation judge and the original settlement offer. Moakley said that agreement was no longer in play. I asked if we had to notify the case judge that the town of Butland had withdrawn the settlement offer he had witnessed.

Moakley said she didn't need to know about the refusal from the town. I told him I hoped he was right. He said that Attorney Kerry Dunn, attorney for the town, had called with another offer of $35,000, and he asked me if I was interested in that offer. He said I would not get a better one, and he advised me to take it. Once again, he was pushing my button, and I was upset with his opinion. I told him that he had all the information on my case that proved that my adversaries were using lies and tricks. Then I asked him if he was also playing tricks with me. Moakley actually said I was incorrigible. He said that I thought that people were against me, but they were not. What was happening was just the way the laws worked. He said it was all about what could be proved in a court of law, and that didn't include hearsay. I told him he was both right and wrong. If he, as my attorney, didn't take the correct facts and evidence forward to the judge, he was wrong. I agreed that he needed the facts and evidence so a judge could make a proper judgment.

The other problem was that Judge Jill Rip-Off had told us she would wait to make her judgment until she had learned the result of the mediation. That was why I had asked Moakley if he had to notify Judge Rip-Off that the town had withdrawn their offer. I told Moakley that I had talked to other attorneys to gain their help me and guidance. He said that was why he called me incorrigible. He said I never stopped looking for problems. I told him I needed an attorney who would not lie. I needed an attorney who would do his job properly and not deceive me or cover up anything that was going on with my cases. We both knew the truth. The town officials and their attorneys were lying about every aspect of the situation. I had been set up by Robert Smith, and the town officials were trying to save their asses. Then I said that, if any medical or legal professionals had falsified my medical or legal records, they had committed federal and state offenses. He told me not to worry—he knew the laws. I said I had known too many liars who had said they knew things, and I had ended up dealing with problems myself many times. I told him I was not afraid of the problems or consequences; that was for other people to worry about. Moakley tried to defuse the situation by saying we should discuss questions we might encounter at the workers' compensation meeting. I excused myself to go to the bathroom.

While I was out of the room, my mother explained to Moakley that her son had lost everything in his life. How did my attorney think I was feeling at that time because of all the lies, deception, and hurt? She suggested I might feel as if I was failing as a man. She said that I had given up my business to work for the town. I had worked conscientiously for twelve years as a plowing contractor, and I had made friends among the town workers during that time. When the town hired me as an employee, I thought that all my troubles would be gone, but that hadn't happened. Instead, I had picked up more significant problems that had pushed me over the edge with mental stress and physical symptoms. Now I was receiving no cooperation from doctors, attorneys, judges, or the letters I had written. My mother told Moakley that she knew I had done my best for the town. She reminded him that, when I was plowing for the town, Robert Smith always complemented my plowing and work ethic. When I showed up before the town employees, Smith would yell at me for getting in before the town workers. She also reminded him that, when I was hired full time at the end of the year, I received compliments from everybody at work about the excellent job I had done on the windows. Then after the new year, everything started to fall apart for me because of one man—Robert Smith. Everybody else was happy with my work.

Later, my mother told me that Moakley had interrupted her and asked why the foremen had complained about my work. My mother told him to think about it. Robert Smith was the main boss of the DPW office. Didn't he think that Smith might have been corrupted or incompetent? Or maybe there was something wrong with the man. She told him that I had come home and told her how Moakley had nailed the two bosses at the depositions and how he had known they were lying. My mother said that Moakley didn't seem to know what to say at that point. She told him that he and I had lost the discrimination case in federal court, and she asked him how that had happened. He didn't even have an answer for that question either. My mother later told me that Attorney Allen Moakley looked pretty bad after she had talked to him. She saw guilt on his face, and she asked him if he had accepted a pay-off of some kind from the town.

When I returned from the bathroom, I noticed the expression on Allen's face and wondered what had happened. I sat down and asked what I should expect from the judge who had treated me like shit the last by making a judgment prematurely. She had said she would wait to hear the results of the mediation, but she had denied me on the day of the hearing. Moakley said he didn't know what to say to me. He said he had news about the offer from the town. He said I had asked for a meeting so we could discuss the case. I told him I had, but he was the attorney, and he must have a plan for presenting this case to the judge. I asked, if we filed an appeal and went to court, would we need witnesses? He said we would. He asked me to name people who would be good witnesses. I looked at him funny and asked what he meant. I told him he was supposed to decide on the people he would need to explain and prove what had happened to me at my job at the DPW office. Then he was supposed to decide which of my family members could best explain my situation at home. Finally, he was supposed to decide which doctors could best explain my health conditions. I asked him why I was giving him direction about how to do his job when he was supposed to be explaining all of that to me and my mother. He, as the attorney, should be putting us at ease with these issues. How could he not understand why I was so upset with him? How could he not understand why I was questioning his job performance? Once again, Attorney Moakley just pushed off the questions and told me to give him a list of people I wanted as witnesses. I told him I could give it to him right then and there, but he said he had to see another client. He told me to email the list of witnesses, and he would see me in Sealand on the designated date. I was upset as we left the office, and my mother said we would speak in the car.

When my mother and I got in the car, I ask what had happened when I was out of the room. Before she answered, I told her that I thought Attorney Moakley was a piece of shit and sucked as an attorney. My mother said she had been so upset with the conversation. She said I had asked the right questions, but Moakley was just not answering them. She said I needed to find another attorney to handle this part of the case. She believed that Moakley would leave me high and dry when I needed him most. I reminded her that he had already done that to me during the discrimination case, and we had lost. I had not had time to find an attorney to help with the appeal to the federal court. My sister Sarah and I had written an appeal within the required ten days, but we had lost that too.

I asked my mother what she and Moakley had talked about, and she said she had told him how bad my health had become while I was fighting doctors, attorneys, town officials, and judges, all the while waiting for responses to all the letters I had written to government officials. She said that was the reason Moakley had an odd expression on his face when I returned to the room. He hadn't expected her to speak up to him about my situation. My mother had told him that I could sue him in court after this was all over.

About a week later, just before court day, I received another bill from Moakley charging me for that visit to his office. I showed my mother and my family members, and they all said that he was overcharging and stealing my retainer money. I said, when it comes to the workers' compensation case, there should be no charge till Moakley won the case.

On the day of the workers' compensation hearing, I showed up with my niece, Jane, and my mother. As usual, Attorney Moakley was late. He checked in with the receptionist, acknowledging that he and his client were there for the hearing. I was still upset with him because of the bill he had sent. And I was angry for many other reasons. Our relationship had become a disaster. After we exchanged greetings, I asked him if he had heard anything from the town attorney, Kerry Dunn. He said he hadn't. I asked him if he knew what would happen at the hearing, and he said he didn't. When I heard his answers, I wanted to kick the shit out of him so bad, but I didn't need to go to jail for stupid, reactionary behavior. Especially where money and a lawsuit were involved, I just wanted this case to end as soon as possible. At that time, unfortunately, I didn't know that the case would carry on for another two years while both attorneys and four judges altogether at the Workers' Compensation Office committed multiple crimes.

Judge Rip-Off called in the two attorneys, and they had their little talk. They prevented me from being in the room with them. My mother and Jane called me over. My mother said that's why our law system is so corrupted—the hearing was about me, but I couldn't hear what they were saying about me or the case. For all we knew, they were making a deal to intentionally cause my case to fail before I had a chance for justice, but because I didn't know about it, it was okay with them. Verbal threats are against the law. The sad thing is that people just don't threaten others for no reason; verbal threats or physical actions are always made for a reason. My adversaries had committed white-collar crimes in both of my cases; all the professionals I had been dealing with were guilty. The verbal and physical threats that were being perpetrated were legal and within the laws of this country. But when anyone accuses professional people of improper behavior, they suddenly mark the accuser as a threat, and they finish off that accuser in some horrible way. The wrong people succeed too many times. I have said that the people have been screwed over so many times and in so many ways—personally and in business—because of gender, color, religion, age, and just about any way that people can discriminate. The sad part is that nobody can understand the hurt and desire for revenge that people experience from the hurt and loss they carry in their minds and hearts. The worst part of our government is that the conspiracists and terrorists are one in the same. Our government divides and conquers the people, and nobody is stopping them from doing as they please as they destroy everything and everybody.

Judge Rip-Off finally called me into the courtroom. My family members accompanied me. Judge Rip-Off started by asking Attorney Moakley if there had been any progress with the case. He said there hadn't. Judge Rip-Off asked Kerry Dunn, attorney for the town of Butland, where the case stood. She asked the judge to dismiss the case again. Judge Rip-Off said that couldn't happen; we needed a solution. Moakley said that we wanted to appeal her decision, and he requested that we be allowed to submit the evaluation of my medical records that had been compiled by an independent doctor. The goal was to clear up questions about me and my health problems. The judge asked if Dunn agreed with this request. She said she had a problem with the request because there was no cause for it. She said that I wasn't sick; I was just lying so I could receive money from the town. The judge asked Dunn if she was medically qualified to make that diagnosis. Was she a doctor or an attorney? The judge asked if there was a reason for her objection. Dunn said she was not at liberty to explain at that time, but it related to their earlier conversation.

Then the judge said she was willing wait for the results of the independent doctor's report. She would take action then. I looked back at my family with a questioning look because I didn't understand what was happening. The judge had said that we needed to have an independent evaluation about my health, and we would go from there. Moakley explained to the judge that I was financially disadvantaged because of the expense of the two cases I was involved in, and we needed the state to cover the cost of the evaluation. The judge said that would be okay. She told him to have me fill out the required paperwork. The judge asked if there were any other matters at that time, and both attorneys said no. But I told the.judge I had something to say.

The judge got upset that I wanted to speak. I told her I would like to know about the conversation she and the attorneys had had before the hearing. I said it seemed to me, from some of the conversation I had heard during the hearing, that some laws were being broken. The judge told me that the conversation was no business of mine. I said I disagreed because, if they were breaking the law and hiding the facts concerning what had been going wrong, that was a problem for everybody involved with this case. I told her that they all thought they could talk around me because I was stupid or mentally challenge, but I was not. From the time I was discriminated against and got fired until that moment, about five years later, people had just been lying, as attorney Dunn had, but I assured her I had not been lying. I said that everybody was just questioning the truth of the mental stress I had endured on the job. They all debated whether it was true without hearing testimony from witnesses who knew the truth. I told them that the facts were right in front of their faces. They were just ignoring them and making up their own rules to fit the case.

Meanwhile, stress-related problems in this country contribute to thing like the marathon bombing, Black Lives Matter, and members of our government acting like children who can't agree on anything for the people. I told her our laws were a joke. I said they didn't want justice. Instead they wanted controversy and problems—divide the people and conquer them later. People who have mental problems are being pushed aside or ignored. I told her that a single man had caused my problem, and they were allowing him to get away with it.

The judge asked if I was finished. I told her not really, but I was finished for the time being. The judge closed the session. I asked Moakley what kind of doctor I would see, and he said that it would be a psychiatrist. I asked him what about a rheumatologist who could explain my fibromyalgia, which was related to my stress problems and pain. I told him that this sort of thing was one of my main problems. Moakley just ignored me again.

CHAPTER 28

THE INDEPENDENT DOCTOR'S
REPORT AND THE PANDEMIC

Two doctors I had not seen before would see me for the independent evaluation. Dr. Green was from the town, and Dr. Weinberg was from the courts. Both appointments had been scheduled so the doctors could finish their reports before the next hearing. I had heard different stories about doctors lying and discrediting medical records to win their cases.

I had my evaluation for the town with Dr. Green in the fall of 2019. I took my niece Jane with me as a witness. Unfortunately, Attorney Kerry Dunn had not sent Dr. Green my medical records and other information (such as Robert Smith's deposition) about the cases so he had no background information.

Why would a doctor need deposition information for a medical evaluation? Attorney Dunn was trying to delay the medical evaluation. As a result, the town evaluation would not be allowed as evidence for the town side. Attorney Dunn argued with Senior Judge Bill Child of the Workers' Compensation Office. Senior

Judge Child had said the law was that, if evidence was not provided by the required date, that information could not be included in the case. He could not allow the law to be broken. Dunn was upset with his answer, but she was also busy looking into hiring an investigation company to follow me around and document the everyday things I did. So, that made it difficult for Dunn to be on time with the medical evaluation. The same situation had been discussed in the last court session during secret talks among the judge and attorneys.

The evaluation with Dr. green was very difficult for me because my anxiety triggered my fibromyalgia pain throughout my whole body. Dr. Green explained that he didn't have the medical records and would evaluate without that information. He didn't explain that he had other information about the cases. He asked me what I thought, in my own words, had happened at my job. When I heard those words, I knew that he was using a psychological approach to break down my guard. The stories that I had heard about this type of doctor were true. As he continued to ask questions, I noticed he was dissecting my story to see if I was lying about my health conditions and my job experiences. I explained that there were witnesses to some of my claims. I also explained that my doctors had written my medical records, not me. I told him I didn't understand what this evaluation was about. As far as my work-related experiences were concerned, that was for a court to decide, not him. As far as my medical records were concerned, he should talk to my doctors for answers, or at least read all the documentation. A judge should be listening to the answers to the questions he was asking, not an independent doctor, especially when he didn't have access to my medical records. I told him that I had been stressed out at my job because one man had bullied me, harassed me, and made discriminating remarks on the job. The people involved in the town side of the dispute were lying about the entire situation, including the attorneys and judges who were involved in trying to protect the town from a lawsuit. I said I would not let that happen; I would prove that the town representatives and Robert Smith lied at the beginning and kept lying as time went on. Everybody involved had lied about the cases. Dr. Green asked if I was sure about my accusations. I said of course I was. Two and a half hours later, after more senseless questions, he finally said that we were finished.

Two weeks later, I received the report from Dr. Green. It consisted of lies and contained nothing that would help us in a courtroom. In a single sentence, he said that I should go to work because I was faking my health problems, and I was lying about my negative experiences with Robert Smith.

I received paperwork about my appointment to see the independent doctor hired by the worker's compensation court, Dr. Weinberg. Once again, I took my niece Jane to the appointment. We arrived early, just as I did with all my appointments. When the doctor told me to sit down and he would see me in a few minutes, my anxiety started, and my fibromyalgia pain kicked in. The stress of attending all the medical and legal appointments and explaining my story and my complaints repeatedly was taking an unbelievable toll on my health—and my life. Dr. Weinberg introduced himself and said that he had been requested by the workers' compensation court to evaluate my medical situation. He asked for a license to prove my identity. Then Dr. Weinberg told me he had read my records, and he wanted me to give him my own version of my problems. He assured me that he was not working for either side of the case; he was just there for an evaluation, so I should be comfortable in being honest. Once again, I noticed how people tried to break my guard and use a psychological approach with the questions they asked. My problem was, however, that my guard was always up because I had been deceived so many times. It had all started with Robert Smith, and then it had continued up to the present time, including doctors, attorneys, judges, and state and federal agencies. It seemed to me that nobody was concerned with my complaints about justice or the laws that were being broken.

I explained my legal problems, health problems, and complaints to Dr. Weinberg. I also took a chance because I decided to trust him. I explained that the whole thing had started in the town of Butland DPW office with a man named Robert Smith—and only him. I explained how Smith had begun by harassing me, then bullying me, then discriminating with me. I told him I had witnesses. Finally, Smith had threatened my job, and I began to get sick with stomach pain. Finally, I was dismissed for being sick. I told him I had both primary and secondary health problems, and I described them. I asked Dr. Weinberg if he knew about fibromyalgia and its effects on the body. He said he did. I told him I experience more secondary symptoms including depression, psychosis, and others that I couldn't think of at the time. But I told him he had my records, so he had access to all my diagnoses. He said he knew about my symptoms from the records. I told him I had seen doctors who said they understood my symptoms but didn't want to cooperate with my attorney. Dr. Weinberg asked me to confirm that my doctors didn't want to cooperate with my attorney and the courts, and I said they didn't. He said that was unheard of and was against state and federal laws.

I explained that, meanwhile, town officials and representatives had been lying about my work ethic and the reason I had been released from my job. Also, my family and I had caught my attorney in lies. I said I was fighting everybody who was protecting the town from having to pay me a settlement because they had been at fault. I told him I had spent about eleven years working hard as a plowing subcontractor to show that I could do good work for the town because I wanted to get full-time employment. The thing that blew my mind was that this one man, whom I had trusted, had turned against me in a heartbeat. I told him that many of my coworkers had warned me that Smith was notoriously bad a boss. I told the doctor that, at the time, I was fifty years old and had never had any problems with my private customers or any job I had worked on in my life, and I believed that was why my negative experiences with Smith had affected me the way they did, causing stress, which caused illness.

We were finished in about forty-five minute; the other evaluation had taken two and a half hours. Dr. Weinberg said he had read my records and talked to me, so he was all set. He would send his report to the court, and a copy to my attorney.

Two weeks later, I called Attorney Moakley and asked about the two doctors' reports. He said he had just received the court doctor's report. When I asked about the town doctor's report, he said he had that one too. I asked about the town doctor's report first, and Moakley said that he called me a faker altogether. I asked how I could have faked my health problems when they are documented by multiple doctors He said he didn't know, but, on the other hand, the court doctor's report was in my favor. Dr. Weinberg had recommended that the town pay me two and a half years of back pay in a workers' compensation settlement. I said that would be wrong because my fibromyalgia would cause me a lifetime of problems and pain. Moakley said I should be happy with what I had just received from that doctor. I said we were in our fifth year of battle, and could not see an end? He explained that we should receive a notice to go to court soon. I reminded him that we wouldn't get a date for about three months. About a week after this conversation with Moakley, however, I received a notice from the Workers' Compensation Office. I was to be there on January 27, 2020.

I went through my medical records from Dr. Jax, our own independent personal doctor who had been hired by Attorney Moakley. Dr. Jax's fee for the evaluation had been the best within my price range, and Moakley had told me that he specialized in fibromyalgia. The price range had been between $3000 and $20,000. Unfortunately, I could not afford the most expensive doctor, but I believe we get what we pay for in services. But I realized, as I went through the report, that it was in favor of my cases. Still, it didn't include information about how the stress problems can lead to secondary problems, and it didn't include information about fibromyalgia and the fact that it is a stress-related problem. I thought about what Moakley had said about Dr. Jax being a specialist in fibromyalgia. There was very little information available about fibromyalgia and how it relates to stress problems. The report from Dr. Jax was okay, but because it didn't include information that fibromyalgia is a stress-related illness, it didn't provide the proof we needed for the workers' compensation case.

On the surface, Moakley's attitude seemed good, but underneath, I knew his job performance as an attorney was not suitable. The worst part of the court ruling was that, once the independent court doctor sent his report to the judge, all other medical records would have no influence on the judge, even if all the records contained the same information, and that include the town doctor's report that had been disqualified because it had not been submitted on time.

I got an email from Moakley asking me to set up a telephone appointment with him. Weeks before Christmas, we talked, and he suggested that we extend the court date. He said that Attorney Dunn had already agreed to prolong the date. He told me that he needed to prepare for the court date, and Dunn also needed extra time. He added that Christmas was coming up and he had made plans to go away on vacation. I said that the two attorneys canceling so many dates and all the other bullshit from everyone involved was crazy. I brought up the fact that Dr. Jax's report had not included anything about the relationship between fibromyalgia and stress. He said that it didn't matter now because all the other records didn't count any more. Attorney Dunn wanted to disqualify the court evaluation. I couldn't believe it! Moakley said he thought it was because the senior judge said he wouldn't accept late documents. But that didn't matter either because the court doctor had the last say with the case now.

I asked Moakley why Attorney Dunn was going out of her way to damage my case criminally. He said he didn't know. I told him that I understood that she had to fight for her clients, but her behavior was too much. My primary complaint was that she had been lying about all the facts. Moakley, my family members, and I had all caught Attorney Dunn in lies. The town representatives were also lying. Just about everyone on the side of the town were either not cooperating or lying. Once again, Moakley said he didn't understand why I was going through so many problems with my cases. I said to Moakley that he had talked to Dunn, so he must see her intentions from her conversation. He said he didn't, but I told him he must because, when attorneys take on cases, they have to feel people out to see if they are lying or playing the attorneys for fools. Moakley said it wasn't like that. I told him that people in business for themselves must have ways of predicting problems. I had done this with my own business with all of the people I dealt with over the years—customers, suppliers, inspectors, workers. So many things can go wrong with construction jobs. Again, Moakley insisted that his job wasn't like that. I saw that I wasn't making any headway with him, so I asked if we were all done. Allen said no; he needed me to agree to extend the court date. I told him it sounded to me as if the plan was already in place, so I had no choice but to agree.

The attorneys canceled the January date for poor reasons. I have always noticed that people don't want to work or pay attention to their jobs as the holidays approach. People who work in government and in private concerns just push off work for as long as possible. But, when it comes to the physical labor jobs, the work always must be done—yesterday.

I received a new appointment for the workers' compensation

hearing. It would be on March 26, 2020, another three months away. This time, a new problem would be develop. The original judge, Jill Rip-Off was leaving her job at the end of 2019. Moakley did not get this information to me right away, and when he did send it to me in an email, I called him and asked him what was going on with that judge. Moakley said that she had resigned her position and taken back her status as a judge. I asked him if there was going to be a conflict of interest with my case, and he said no. I said this situation seemed strange to me, and I asked him if she had left for personal reasons. He said she hadn't. I asked what would happen to the case now, and he said we'd get a new judge. I said we would be starting all over with the new judge, and he said we would be indeed. I asked if we would need a new date, but he said the March 26 date was still valid.

When March 2020 rolled around, however, the world was in a panic because of the corona virus disease, also known as COVID-19, which had started in China and then run rampant across the globe.

This pandemic changed the world as we all knew it. Some people believed that the virus had been invented by our governments and secret societies worldwide. Our world is overpopulated, and some people believed that governments were using the virus as a way of decreasing world population by natural causes. The sad part about death is that, no matter the cause, death never discriminates against any human—or any life form for that matter. But when government leaders tell the people of the world that they are fighting for the right for everyone's well-being, that is the biggest lie from any government or leader. The world's governments and secret societies have a problem with the direct killing of people because the people of the world would revolt against those who carried out such mass extinction. So that's why they all invented a virus. In the 1300s, the Black Death was a plague caused naturally by fleas and rats on the European continent. The plague caused the death of up to two million people. These problems of uncleanliness sufficient to start a similar plague are unheard of in today's world. Our governments and secret societies are running our world right out of existence. Wars now include threats of nuclear, biological, and chemical weapons. And their waste will contaminate our environment. Now a virus had been released by governments and secret societies along with scientists who didn't even know what they were doing to our world's population. The people of our world are suffering because leaders are killing all of us. The part that doesn't make any sense is that, once all the ordinary people die, what are the rich, famous, and influential government leaders going to do for common labor and other everyday lifestyle requirements? They will have to do everything for themselves.

The pandemic caused so much pain, confusion, loss of life, and insecurity. These problems happen when false governments and secret societies run the world. Government officials and representatives lie and make empty promises to the world's people, and one of the top leaders is the United States government.

There is another virus known as the American government. That organization took land from the proper people—the American Indians. Our country was incorporated in 1776 and, at this writing, has been in existence for 246 years. Our government has divided the people and conquered the people of America and many other countries over time. The government has put the young against the old, color against color, religion against religion. But should the virus have been the last straw that broke the camel's back? Our country was down for just about two years, from March 2020 to September 2022. People have suffered a multitude of negative consequences from this pandemic: isolation during lockdown, the forced wearing of masks, food and household supply shortages, not being able to be with loved ones during life-changing events like birth and death. The children have irreparably lost schooling time, which will have long-reaching negative consequences in level of knowledge and also in socialization. The country was divided by leaders who hid as they stopped people from living normal lives. The common workers were on the front line during the pandemic, trying to hold on to their jobs and help out the population. The pandemic stopped all the governments from doing their jobs. Court cases were cancelled, and justice for our country and the people was stalled. These consequences led to January 6, 2021, when a group people, tired of a government that couldn't do its job right, protested by descending on the US Capitol. I believe we will be discovering for a long time the negative effect the pandemic and the way it was handled has had on our country and the world.

CHAPTER 29

PRIVATE INVESTIGATOR

Attorney Moakley sent me an email in which he asked me if I had been working! I showed my mother and Jane the email, and we all flipped out. I accused the town representatives and Attorney Kerry Dunn of lying and inciting a scandal to throw my case off its tracks. In other words, they were guilty of obstruction of justice and conspiracy with regard to my workers' compensation case. I told my mother and Jane that this was proof that my adversaries had been tampering with the truth, the evidence, and the facts of the case. Town officials and attorneys were fouling both cases with malicious intent. I asked Jane to record my phone call and put my phone on speaker so that she and my mother could listen and witness my conversation with Moakley about these lies.

When I called Moakley, he picked up right away. I asked him calmly what was going on with the case. He said that the town had video and written reports that proved I was working for a company. I asked him what he was talking about. He asked if I had seen the videos or the reports, and I said no. He said he would send them to me. I asked him if he had looked at them, and he said yes. I asked if he had seen me in the videos. He said he had. I told him he may have seen a man in the video, but it wasn't me! He hesitated, and that was all I needed. I freaked out. I wanted to kill him. I yelled at him and told him he'd been working with me for six years, and he didn't know what my face looked like! I had also known Kerry Dunn, the town attorney, so she should be able to recognize me too. I asked Moakley if he trusted me, and he said he didn't.

I was thinking to myself that I should just go along with this information from Moakley. Then I said, since he believed I was the one in the videos, he should tell Attorney Dunn to initiate a perjury case against me, and he could do the same. He told me to wait a minute and explain what I meant. I told him he had said he believed that I was the man in the videos, and I asked him if that was right. He said he wasn't sure. I told him that didn't matter. The town attorney had drummed up this situation of lies. I told him again to tell her to file charges against me, and we would deal with her lies and prove that these two cases against me had been based on lies from the beginning. Allen said he couldn't tell her that. I asked what if I admitted I'd been working and the videos were correct. He said I could not do that. He said I had to look at the videos and read the reports first. I asked him why. I knew that I hadn't worked in any way for anybody. I didn't need to prove anything to myself. I also had family members who could vouch that, except for medical and legal appointments, I had pretty much been at home every day and every night since the whole thing started in 2014. Moakley told me to look at the videos and reports and call him back.

When I hung up the phone, my mother and Jane asked what the fuck was going on between this town attorney, Dunn, and Moakley. I said that was how it had been from the beginning with everybody involved with the cases. They had all been lying from the start.

Jane finally received the videos on the file transfer service Dropbox, and I asked Jane to play them so we could see what new lies were being distributed. While Jane did that, I printed the reports. When I read the reports, I noticed two separate dates: November 24, 2019, and July 4, 2020. The company that had produced the reports was Professional Private Eyes Inc., and they were located in Rhode Island.

The owner of the company, Pert Chanelle, had issued the reports for Attorney Kerry Dunn. The investigation company had placed multiple employees at different scenes to supposedly follow me. The report outlined how the company had conducted its investigation and received information about my family members and me. The company had looked into records at the Butland town hall with regard to property ownership and vehicle registration. They had used Internet social media searches to gather information. The company had done its job almost correctly, but the problem was that they had the wrong people, so the reports and videos were false. This company found my brothers and sister; my mother; my daughter; and my sister's boyfriend, Fred DeMello, who was an owner of a landscape company. The investigation company stated that there were no vehicles registered in my name, and the last vehicle registered in my name was registered in 2017. I had a Facebook account. I had uploaded some pictures of me, but I had not added any new information. They looked up my business and found that the last time I had been active in my company was in 2012. The investigation company could not find me because I was always in my house with health problems.

The videos were real, but they showed only the faces of Fred, my sister Sarah, and other workers in Fred's company. Both videos were of Fred and Fred's company at work; the professional private eyes from this investigation company had reported on and videoed the wrong people! The worst part was that they had looked up my Facebook page and used the picture I had posted there. The bottom line was that this company had lied in their written reports and videos. My whole family and my girlfriend freaked out at the false allegations in these reports and videos.

I started to think about the whole situation and how Attorney Dunn and Attorney Moakley had engaged in their secret little conversations when we were at the workers' compensation hearing the last time. Then I explained to my family members that these videos and reports were the secret weapons of the judge and attorneys who knew that an investigation company would be involved. I knew I was being set up for failure when there was no just cause. I labeled the whole thing a conspiracy act of a white-collar crime. The plan had been started by Dunn at court, and then it passed through the judge and my attorney, Allen Moakley.

My family members and girlfriend said they remembered the professionals in the courtroom referring in front of us to the "secret" talk they had had minutes before. The only problem was that I didn't have physical proof that conversation had occurred. Still, it was obvious that they all were talking to one another—the investigation company, the town representatives, Attorney Dunn, the judge. Even Moakley was involved in the conspiracy, which was a criminal act.

The next day, I call Moakley and told him I'd seen the videos and read the reports. I asked him again if he believed that it was me in the videos, and he said yes again. Then he said that he wanted to withdraw from my case. I couldn't believe what I was hearing. I told him that, if he did that, I would file a lawsuit against him and everybody involved in my cases. Something dirty was going on with both cases.

Then Moakley said that Dunn was going to obtain a warrant to look at Fred's payroll accounts. I told him that he and she were both wrong about me working. I told him he should be able to see that it was not me in the video. The reports and videos all referred to my sister and Fred, and not to me. I told him I didn't have long hair and tits. Neither did I have a heavy-set body. I have a skinny frame. I have short hair and a goatee! Nobody in the videos looked remotely like me! He said again that Dunn was getting a warrant to examine Fred's company records, and he added that he also wanted to talk to Fred and hear from him that I hadn't worked for him. I told him to go ahead and talk to Fred.

Fred set up a time for a phone conversation with Moakley so Moakley could ask him questions about me working for him. Moakley called my phone, and I handed the phone to Fred. Moakley started asking questions about me, but Fred interrupted him and said he'd like to explain before answering any questions. He told Moakley that he had seen the videos and reports. He said that both the reports and the videos were about him and my sister, Sara, along with a few other of his employees. The investigations company had picked up the two trucks in his driveway and followed them to his shop. He insisted that those two vehicles were registered to Sarah and him, and they had nothing to do with me. Then he said that, as far as me working for him, it never, ever happened. He said that insurance and employment laws required him to report any staffing changes. He wasn't about to hire me and take a chance by breaking the law and getting in trouble.

Moakley said that Fred had answered all the questions he'd been planning to ask, but the town attorney, Dunn, still wanted to subpoena Fred's records and mine. Fred said he had spoken to his attorney and had been advised that he didn't have to cooperate with Dunn or the town representatives. Fred then told Moakley that Moakley was hurting me with his words and the games he had been playing with me. Moakley didn't have an answer, and he finally ended the interview.

The day after the phone call with Fred, I copied my bank statements for Moakley, and I sent them to him by email. He responded by saying that I had only about four dollars in the bank. I responded, saying that I hadn't had any money since the start of my legal and health problems, all caused by the town. I told him I had no money at all. I asked him what he was doing about the false accusations. I asked him if we could report them to the proper authorities. I never got an answer to that question. I still think that Moakley was hiding the truth so it could not contribute to justice. Attorney Dunn sent Fred paperwork requesting his records. She also tried to call Fred to talk with him, but he refused to accept her calls.

Moakley sent me an email about the new judge at the Workers' Compensation Office, Betty MacDuff. I thought I might write an email to this judge and explain the problems I was seeing with the two attorneys and the false reports and videos.

CHAPTER 30

LETTER TO THE NEW JUDGE, CALLING OTHER ATTORNEYS FOR ADVICE AND TO TAKE OVER THE CASE

In my first letter to Judge Betty Macduff, I complained the entire. I told her about the attorneys who would appear before her on the date of my hearing. I also sent the same letter to Senior Judge Bill Child so he would have input about my complaints and problems.

I wanted to expose my complaints about the criminal acts involved in the both the workers' compensation case and the discrimination case because all the people involved in the two cases tied them both together. My information would provide an opportunity for the two judges to take action together, find the truth about my complaints and problems, and then take action on any criminal actions.

In my letter, I explained that witnesses were being involved in a cover-up, false reports had been issued from the beginning, starting with reports from the town of Butland and ending with the false written reports and videos from a private investigator hired by

Attorney Dunn. I explained that Attorney Moakley had knowledge of these reports. I told them that Attorney Moakley had not been correctly representing me as an attorney. I told them about the abuse had I received as a result of allegations from the town. I told them about the false allegations made by the two attorneys. I explained how my health problems had started because of my experiences while I was employed by the town and had been exacerbated because I was receiving no cooperation from anyone involved with my cases. I also included complaints about the previous judge, Jill Rip-Off. I questioned why she had left her job and the case, knowing that the case would be continued with a new judge. I asked if something related to my case had stopped her from continuing her work in the Workers' Compensation Office. I gave them all this information and reassured them that most of my records and videos would prove that I was telling them the truth.

In return, both judges responded that my letters were not the proper way of handling these problems. They told me that my attorney should address these issues.

Then I wrote an email to both judges saying that the complaints included complaints against my attorney as well as elements in the entire case, and I needed help with my problems with the two cases and everybody involved.

Two weeks later, I received an email from Judge Betty MacDuff. She had sent my letters to Attorney Moakley and Attorney Dunn. Her excuse was that they needed to know everything that was going on with the case. I also received an email from Senior Judge Bill saying that he couldn't get involved with my cases.

I showed these emails to my mother and family members. My mother told me I was beating my head against a rock, and I could not change the corruption in our laws and in the people who were in charge as leaders. Unfortunately, she told me, I'd had a lot of bad luck with both of my cases. It had started with Robert Smith and continued with doctors, attorneys, judges. So many lies had been told by so many professional people. My mother told me I should be careful about my health. She said she didn't want anything more to happen to me. I told her that I was only fighting for the principle of the matter. Everything that had happened to me had adversely affected the rest of my life—my health, my finances, my work opportunities. My mother advised me to try to find another attorney to handle the case. I said I would start calling attorneys.

The pandemic affected my workers' compensation case as it did so many legal cases throughout the country. The pandemic stopped people from going to work and to school, and just about everything else. The only people who did work were essential people like the police, fire fighters, medical professionals, and people who worked in stores. All levels of courts were closed, which made it difficult to process new crimes or cases that were in process when the pandemic started.

It was difficult to talk to attorneys because they were staying at home on lockdown with their families. The world was at a standstill for a long time. Things would slowly move forward in time, but my case was held up for a long time. In time, some court procedures were handled through virtual meetings. The people who had committed crimes were connected using computers of the prison systems, and everyone else used personal computers.

My case was partially addressed in virtual meetings and emails. I was able to remain in the safety of my home. To most people, any kind of court procedure can be very stressful, especially if they are already having stress problems. One of my problems with these virtual meetings was that I had an old computer. I had to borrow an updated computer. Then, being computer illiterate didn't help out; I was not familiar with all the new technology.

When I started to call attorneys, I left messages. I didn't even hear from about 75 percent of them, and of the 25 percent I did hear from, half took the time to listen and the other half said they were not interested in the case. Most of the ones who did listen explained that the main problem was that no attorney wanted to pick up a case with all types of problems. Some told me I and my cases had been blackballed. To them it sounded intentional. One told me that my case had been doomed from the beginning because of the power held by the town officials. They told me that my doctors should have cooperated with my attorney, and it was questionable if my attorney had done everything correctly with the doctors. One said that, from the way I had explained my situation with my attorney, he had neglected his responsibilities with me. He told me I had proof with all my records. My attorney could be disbarred and sent to prison. Another attorney said that the town attorney and my attorney could be disbarred for falsifying records. The judges knew that all the attorneys were doing things wrong with the cases.

My attorney, another said, should not cooperating have gone back to the doctors and told them that they could be held responsible for withholding medical information on a legal matter. The therapist could be held accountable for her actions because she believed the computerized questionnaire instead of relying on her experience and understanding that I would not hurt myself or anyone else.

I learned that it was the judge's job to oversee the entire case and understand when attorneys were abusing their powers. They had to take time to listen to me as the subject of the case. One attorney said that my entire case was bogus, and I needed to start writing to my senators, the district attorneys of Suffolk and Norfolk counties, the governor and attorney general of Rhode Island, the Justice Departments in Sealand and Washington, the FBI in Sealand, and the news media. I had to try to get my story out and then look for some justice in the process. Then the attorney said that my case was too big for me to handle; I needed a large law firm to address all the different problems and areas involved with my cases.

I told the attorney that I had already written letters to all the people he had suggested writing to, but no one had been willing to show any interest let alone help me. Or they said it was not their job. The attorney told me to keep after them. I told him that anyone who makes a complaint should be taken seriously and not ignored. He agreed and said that our government is ineffective when government employees and representatives don't do their jobs properly, and I agreed with him. The attorney wished me good luck with my heavy burden before he said good-bye.

I also talked to other attorneys who made the same observations and gave me the same advice. They all agreed with the simple fact that it's a shame that I was going through such a tough time, but I needed to argue the cases for myself until someone stepped up to help me to attain justice. They advised me that I had a more significant task than I realized, and it was a shame what our government and laws were doing to the people of this country.

CHAPTER 31

LETTERS TO ALL THE
PROPER AUTHORITIES—AGAIN

I STARTED WRITING LETTERS AGAIN TO ALL THE PROPER LAW enforcement, legal authorities, and government authorities explaining my complaints of criminal actions involving my cases and the professional people handling my medical and legal problems. I never had any response from anyone I wrote to.

I wrote the first letters to the Rhode Island governor and the attorney general, the FBI in Sealand, four television news stations in Sealand, and the two Sealand newspapers. In my letters, I explained my health problems and my legal problems. I explained how the town of Butland had wrongfully dismissed me because I was sick even though my absence from work was backed up doctor's notes to comply with the town rules. I explained the discrimination I had experienced from Superintendent Robert Smith of the Butland DPW office—the bullying, harassment, and threats to my job when I was sick because of stress caused by Superintendent Robert Smith's treatment of me.

Smith had never explained why he had dismissed me from my job, but after I obtained an attorney, the lies began to come out about my discharge from employment by the town. Smith would do anything to save his job and avoid a lawsuit. This man and town representatives terrorized me for no reason, and they showed their power as bullies by using lies and deceit. I explained that my doctors admitted I had stress-related health problems, but they would not tell the complete truth; they refused to connect the stress to my job experiences. Also, they wouldn't commit to saying that my health would get worse over time. The doctors would not cooperate with my attorney, Allen Moakley, or the courts in any way, and they were breaking the law. Additionally, Attorney Moakley had not been properly defending me according to the law. I had caught him lying, as had some of my members of family. Whenever I confronted him with his lies, he would just ignore the situation altogether. He refused to use all the information I passed along to him, and I felt this was neglect. I also explained that Smith and the town officials along with my doctors and my attorney were only adding more stress to my life, which was causing increased health problems.

In addition to the letters, I took the time to visit the offices of the FBI in Sealand and the offices of the district attorney in Norfolk to file formal complaints about my entire story. When I visited the FBI office, I felt as if I was walking into a fortress because of all the security checks I had to go through. When I finally spoke to an FBI agent, he listened to my story and my complaints, and then he explained that the town of Butland was under surveillance because of other complaints. I asked what would happen with my complaint, and he said they would look into my problems, but I would never hear from them. When I visited the Norfolk district attorney's office for the first time, they sent several people to listen to my complaints, and I explained the whole story to them. They were sympathetic, but they said that they could not help me with my situation. I asked where I should go to have my complaints addressed and get results, and they weren't sure what office to send me to. I said thank you when I left, but I observed to Jane that I couldn't believe that the FBI and district attorney offices couldn't help the people in any way, but they expect citizens to report crimes and to cooperate with them in their investigations. In fact, people could be arrested for not cooperating with them. Jane observed that the government issues conflicting information. And that was just one of many problems with our government.

The second time I dealt with the Norfolk district attorney office, I called and asked if I could talk to them and explain all the growing problems caused by my cases. At that point, I wanted to add the problems the judges were causing. When I spoke to the assistant district attorney, Sam Crow, I asked for a meeting so I could explain my problems. I said I could bring some of my records to show the proof of my problems. Assistant District Attorney Sam Crow said that I should make copies of my papers and drop them off with the secretary at the front desk. He would look over the information and call me back with a response. I tried to explain my situation over the phone, but he said I had to put my information in a letter and include it with my papers. I asked him how long he would need to go over the papers, and he said about a week. About two weeks after I dropped off my files and letter, I received a call from Crow. He explained that my case wasn't something the district attorney's office would deal with. I asked where I should go to get results. I told him that no one had responded to my pleas for help. He said he had read the information I had sent. He said he sympathized with me, but there was nothing he could do about my troubles. He suggested I try contacting the Suffolk district attorney office in Sealand.

I also went to the police station in Butland to ask for assistance. When I got there, the desk officer asked what I needed, and I explained that I wanted to report a white-collar crime. The officer said he would call someone to take my report. When the officer showed up, we went into a room, and he asked what he could do for me. I said that I wanted to report a white-collar crime that started in 2014 and was continuing to the present time. It concerned my job at the DPW office in Butland. And it concerned doctors, attorneys, and judges who didn't have the truth from the attorneys. I told him the doctors were not complying with the attorneys, the judges, and the courts. The police officer told me I should report this to the state police. I said that would be like going into the lion's den, and I couldn't do that because my stress-related health problems would only worsen; it would be like returning to the crime scene. A police officer said that, because of where the problem started, I could contact the Norfolk and Suffolk district attorney offices. I said that I lived in Butland, and it also started here. The officer said that was the best he could do for me at that time. I said I would take his advice and contact the district attorney offices.

I also thought I should report the crimes to the state police in Milton. When I got there, I explained that I wanted to report a crime, and the desk officer said he would send someone out to help me. As I was waiting, I remembered that the state police had a section on their website about white-collar crimes, which is why I was there trying another avenue. When the state police officer came out, we went into a room, and I explained the problems. He said that I needed to go to the district attorney's office in Norfolk County. I asked if the state police dealt with white-collar crimes, and he said yes, but the investigation had to go through the district attorney offices. I told him I had already been to the at the district attorney's office, and I had been told that they don't deal with white-collar crimes.

I wrote to the Department of Justice in Washington DC because their website stating that white-collar crimes would not be tolerated in our country. I sent two separate letters at different times and got no reply to either letter. I sent all my letters by certified mail that required a signature. I sent letters to the *Washington Post* and the *New York Times*. I did not get any reply from them either. Signature cards didn't even come back from the last round of letters sent out to the Suffolk district attorney's office and the *Washington Post*. I kept careful records of all my transactions, and I was amazed when a simple return signature card didn't come back to me. That meant that the United States Post Office was tampering with the signature cards.

I even wrote letters to two Rhode Island senators near the end of the workers' compensation case. I had always heard their claims that they were in office to help the public in need, but I didn't even get a reply from their offices. It's a sad day when citizens try to follow all the laws of this country and nobody wants to deal with their problems or the crimes committed against them.

Government employees, especially law enforcement employees, ignore complaints against people in similar positions to their own from citizens because they want to protect those in power. We, as citizens, have no choice but to accept the screwing we receive from our government.

I will not give up the fight for fair and equal justice for victims of white-collar crimes and many other areas of crimes that citizens have complained about for many years. I have been educated that the pen is mightier than the sword in today's world, but in the old days, it was the opposite: the sword was mightier than the pen. On the streets, guns are mightier than people, and this is how our government and law enforcement will treat us if it comes down to citizens fighting for our rights. It is ironic that military tactics could be used to divide and conquer the people. Still, our government is doing that very thing to the public. A good example is the COVID-19 pandemic when so many rules conspired to control the population. What will come of our world when false leaders lie and deceive and do anything as they please to further their own goals?

I bumped into an old friend, Norman Lake, who was an attorney. After we chatted for a bit, I told him I was involved in a legal case that was giving me problems. Norman Lake said that was a shame, and he asked why I hadn't called him first. I told him I hadn't thought about him because of my health problems. Norman told me to come by his office, and he would try to help me with my case. First thing next morning, I went go to Lake's office in Butland. At his suggestion, I explained my entire story. He said I should have gone to him first. And he said that, if I gave him all the information from the discrimination case, he would look it over and tell me if the outcome had been legal. The cost would be about $1,500. I asked if he would also be interested in evaluating the workers' compensation case. He said not on a legal level, but he was willing to help me with it if possible. When I asked him why he wouldn't look at on the legal level, he said I already had worked with two attorneys, and it sounded to him as if the town could have been bribing them from the beginning. And that was aside from all the "tricks" that had been intentionally carried out by the town officials and all the attorneys.

He said that the false letter from the foreman and the false reports and videos from the private investigation company proved that I was the victim of a setup. My adversaries had the judges in their pockets, and I had lost. He said I needed to secure a monetary settlement and get out for now. Then I could go back and tell my story through the proper channels of law. I asked if he wanted me to break the law. He said no! I could use the settlement money to finance the publication of a book about my story. The book could provide public support and could encourage an investigation on federal and state levels. Without their involvement, I had no recourse. He told me, if I had a computer, I should start writing. He said it would take time, but I had been involved in a terrible situation with this town and all the attorneys, judges, and doctors. He had never heard of the plaintiff not being heard in court—never!

CHAPTER 32

EMAILS TO WORKERS' COMPENSATION, SENIOR JUDGE AND CASE JUDGE

I THOUGHT ABOUT THE WAY EVERYTHING HAD UNFOLDED, BRINGING me to the worst time in my life. I had tried to follow the law by writing letters and filing complaints with the proper authorities, and I had received no results. I then thought about the reports and videos that contained nothing by lies that had been instigated by the town of Butland and Attorney Kerry Dunn. I thought about Attorney Moakley being willing to accept their lies and not being willing to fight to expose them. I believed I was the victim of a setup, and people were sabotaging my case intentionally. If so, this would also be considered conspiracy, malicious intent, collusion, obstruction of justice, among other illegal activities. These acts break the laws of this country and compromise people's rights.

I wanted to prove that all the people involved with my cases had been breaking the law and destroying my cases. I also believed that, if we could prove that the letter from the foreman was false, the two cases could be reopened. I believed that I had all the evidence and witnesses, but nobody wanted to hear that the laws were being broken by the people who enforced those same laws.

I decided to try another way of following our laws and writing to the new judge and the senior judge at the Workers' Compensation Office. I would try to show them proof by providing evidence and explaining that witnesses who knew the truth were being withheld from providing their information.

I sent emails again to Judge Betty MacDuff and Senior Judge Bill Child to explain that, from the beginning, my workers' compensation case and my discrimination case had been mishandled. I believed that criminal investigations were needed. I explained how the town representatives and all the attorneys were destroying my original complaints and story by manipulating my words and my medical and legal information. I wrote that I needed their help in exposing the entire problem to everybody involved with the cases. I also explained that the attorneys had implicated Judge MacDuff and her office along with Senior Judge Bill Child in criminal actions with regard to my cases. I said that those attorneys were involved in a conspiracy, and they were guilty of malicious intentions, collusion, obstruction of justice. I also explained that I was just trying to follow legal procedures to report criminal interference by the town, the attorneys, and the doctors. Finally, I explained that both cases had been bogus from the beginning as had everybody who was involved. I provided all my contact information so they could get in touch with me and help me to resolve these problems.

About two weeks later, I finally heard from the two judges. Senior Judge Child let me know that illegal goings on did not happen in his office. He told me I wasn't following the proper procedures, and a case judge was handling the case and connected problems. Judge Betty MacDuff responded to me and also sent her response to the senior judge, Attorney Dunn, and Attorney Moakley. She explained that she was sending my email in which I had complained that they had been involved in criminal activities when working on my two cases. She said that I had claimed that witnesses were being hidden, doctors and attorneys were covering up medical and legal information. She said that I had implicated her and her office in these illegal activities. She said she would not tolerate such complications from anyone in her courtroom. She told me that I should address my emails to only the attorneys. She told me to respect her courtroom and her as a judge. She said I should have my attorney handle my problems; it was not proper for me to expect her to do that.

I showed my mother and family members the two emails sent to me by the judges. They couldn't understand why the judges would not help me. I had been following the laws and reporting the crimes. Their thoughts were supported by all the people outside the cases who had told me they believed that the system and people were screwing me. My family members said the judges were pushing the problems off to hide the cracks in the system. That meant that there would be no answers or justice for me.

My mother told me to sit down and calm down. She said that I needed to let this problem go because of my present and future health conditions. She said nothing was important enough that I should risk my health or my life pursuing it. She knew I would not usually back down from a legal or medical fight or anything else in this world, but she believed I didn't have a choice this time. I thanked them for being such a caring family, but I asked how I would take care of myself without a job. I needed finances and a home. I had always paid my way in life. If I borrowed money, how would I pay it back?

My mother said that my problems affected everyone around me, and I needed to let them go. She said that Lisa had told me to quit the battle. In fact, everyone in the family agreed at this point. My mother believed that I should not challenge the judges and attorneys and doctors. That was a big mistake I was making, and I could end up in jail. I told her that I would not go to jail for challenging people who were cheating; I would be fine. I told her that was the reason professional people always got away with breaking the law and bullying the common people. The people give up because they are afraid of the consequences. Nobody in this world should ever be afraid of anyone or anything. I told her I just needed someone to listen to my complaints as I had explained them originally. If those complaints were wrong, I would give up, but I knew they were not wrong, and I had rights as a citizen.

I sent an email response to both judges in answer to their response to my previous email. I told them that I had sent them a whistle-blowing letter about a case they were handling and another case. In return, they sent my email to the very attorneys that I was complaining about. I had asked the judges for help regarding criminal actions that were happening with my cases. I could incriminate both judges in the illegal actions the attorneys had taken. I couldn't believe the judges were paying me back the way they were. I told them I was very disappointed with them because they had lied to protect criminals. I never got a response from either judge. For the time being, I let it go.

I became angry when Moakley did nothing about the false reports and videos provided by the private investigation company. I wrote another email to Judge MacDuff explaining these false allegations and the conduct of my attorney and the town attorney. I explained to Judge MacDuff that Attorney Dunn had presented false reports to Attorney Moakley that supposedly showed that I had been working. I told her the videos were of my sister, her boyfriend, and the people who worked for him in his landscaping company. Both attorneys had met me multiple times in person and had a photo of me from my social media pages, so they should have known that I was not the person in that video. When I had looked at the videos myself, I believed that the information from the private investigation company was provided to sabotage my case with her, Judge MacDuff. It was a similar strategy used by the discrimination attorney, Stoneman, had used with his false letter from foremen Scott at the DPW office. I asked her what she intended to do with those lies. When I finish the email, I also sent it to Attorney Dunn, Attorney Moakley, and Senior Judge Child. I never heard anything about this email from anyone; they all ignored it. Once again, that was criminal action, and it now involved judges in the Workers' Compensation Office. Also in this letter, I asked when we would have a hearing date. The pandemic was still affecting the court system. I never got an answer to these emails.

Attorney Moakley sent multiple motions that he wanted to drop out of the case; this time was within legal procedures. We would have another video hearing about him dropping the case. Attorney Dunn sent in all types of motions saying that her clients were upset with this new development. Her clients had spent large amount of money to defend these cases, and they wanted it to stop. She also asked again that the case be dismissed. The judge told everyone these issues would be addressed in a video meeting.

We received notice of a video meeting time and date by email within a week. On the day of the meeting, I was the first one online. The judge's secretary came on next, and then Moakley, who explained that he was once again on vacation. Finally, Dunn came on saying she had almost forgotten about the meeting. After we all checked in, the judge came online and asked Moakley to present his motions. He explained that his client had written letters complaining about his services, and he believed that I wanted to represent myself and move ahead without an attorney. If he continued to represent me, he could be incriminated with regard to these two cases. The judge asked Dunn to explain the motions. She said her clients wanted the case dismissed, but the judge said that was not possible. Dunn said that, if Moakley was allowed to be dropped from the case, the case would drag on until I retained a new attorney. She said that I was not capable because of my mental problems to represent myself. But Judge MacDuff said that she knew I could write interesting emails, so she thought I was capable of handling my side of the case, but I could not represent myself as well as an attorney could because I did not know the law. Moakley interrupted and said that I was capable mentally, but I had a stress problem. He said I wasn't violent; I just got sick when I was in stressful situations and often had to be rushed to the hospital, and an incident like that could hold up the case.

The judge asked me if I had anything to say. I said that I did, and I told her she hadn't addressed the claims I had sent to her via email concerning the false private investigator reports and videos. I knew they were a big problem. I said that Moakley wanting to drop out because his involvement could incriminate him only showed that he was guilty of inadequately representing me. The town attorney, who had upheld all the problems from the beginning, was now responsible for false reports and videos, but she had the nerve to call me crazy when I was suffering from stress-related symptoms. Judge MacDuff said she would take my comments under advisement, and she would have an answer in a week, at which time we would have another video meeting.

In a week, we had another video meeting. Those present were Judge MacDuff, Attorney Dunn, Attorney Moakley, and me. Judge MacDuff began with Moakley's motion to drop out of the case, and she agreed. Dunn started to say something, but the judge stopped her told her she would have to just deal with the situation. I would be representing myself. She said we would go forward with a hearing date as soon as the governor gave the all-clear for the courts to open again. The judge asked Dunn if she had anything else to say, and she said she didn't. Then the judge asked me if I was going to get an attorney to deal with the court case. I said no because, although I had been trying for a long while, I hadn't been successful in finding anyone to replace Moakley. Judge MacDuff strongly suggested that I hire an attorney for the workers' compensation case. Moakley interrupted to say that I had the right to defend myself. The judge said she wanted me to have an attorney. She said it was too difficult for a citizen to try that sort of case without an attorney. I told the judge I didn't want to delay the hearing date. The judge told me I had lost my attorney, and she wanted me to find a new one. I asked her if she was going to deal with the questions I had asked in my emails. I said that my case was being sabotaged by Attorney Dunn and now by her. I told her that the case would now drag on forever. She asked if I was finished, and I said I was. She told me to give her an update by email when I had found a new attorney.

I sent an email to the senior judge complaining about the case judge and her actions during our meetings. I explained that I had written emails to both of them about all the corruption involved with my cases. I said his email response was that that sort of thing didn't happen in his courtroom and office, but that was a lie, and I had provided evidence. Then I had told them about the false reports and videos that supposedly proved that I had been working. I said I wanted to know what he was going to do with all that information. The next day I received an email from the senior judge. He said I was harassing him and Judge MacDuff, and he could put in a complaint against me for that crime. He said I had an attorney to deal with these problems. If I kept harassing the judges, he would call for an investigation and press charges.

When I received this email, I went on a rampage in my room. I was so pissed off that I wrote back and told him to go ahead and report my letters to the cops. I didn't care. Maybe I would get justice then when the police heard about the legal problems I had been complaining about for years. I told him that he could then be judged by his peers in court, and he could see how that felt. In his return email, the judge used a better tone, but he didn't address any of the problems I had expressed to him about the case or Judge MacDuff. In other words, everyone was ignoring all my complaints on all levels, and they were ignoring each other.

CHAPTER 33
MENTAL ABUSE AND FIBROMYALGIA

Many people in this country complain about physical abuse and mental abuse. The results of physical abuse are very noticeable, and nobody can deny that it has happened. However, when it comes to mental abuse, which causes no obvious physical signs, perpetrators nearly always deny that it has happened. The scary thing is that we all mentally abuse each other at one time or another, either intentionally or accidentally. Sometimes we don't even know that we are hurting the other person. This mental abuse happens in our families and at our workplaces. Sometimes mental abuse happens because of people's status in life, and this can include disabilities, race, age, culture, nationality, and religion. We should all be ashamed of any physical and mental abuse to people. I believe we are all equal. Unfortunately, we live in a world of abuse that comes from every angle possible, and many people get hurt every day from all types of abuse.

The problem of abuse starts with the nation's president as the teacher of the world, and then it rolls through all the branches of our government. The abuse enters businesses and follows to the parents of children who are the only innocent ones. They are abused without a chance for justice. Even animals are abused. Russia is the best example of the worst at the present time because of their war on Ukraine. But people in the rest of the world who stand by and allow the ignorance of killing innocent men, women, and children should face the same consequence Russia experiences. We are in the year 2022, and our government says that we are civilized people, but current events prove that we, as a world, are not civilized. People in Ukraine are being abused. Ukrainians are directly fighting for their lives and rights while other people watch the abuse from the sidelines. War will always affect all the people of the world in some way. Wars are evidence of physical and mental abuse. It is wrong to teach people that war is okay; the abuse and loss of life causes lifelong trauma for everyone involved on every level. We, as world citizens, should never allow wars to destroy our people and our lands. War should be outlawed forever in all the countries of our world.

When I started my business, I noticed that I had the qualities of a leader, and I used that talent as I handled customers, suppliers, and workers. I tried to show that I cared when I dealt with people, and this, added to my knowledge of construction work, helped me be successful. I learned that it takes a strong person to be in charge of other people. Business leaders cannot make mistakes because those mistakes can hurt people; indeed, mistakes can cause them to lose their homes and belongings or even their health and their lives. The most incredible honor anyone can receive is the trust of people who believe in you. In my construction work, I learned that it takes a lot of hard work and knowledge to be successful, but it isn't always easy being a leader. I had to look out for everybody on the job. The workers were always a challenge because of drinking, drugs, and poor work habits. I had to learn who could be trusted. I learned to set an example and show my employees the proper way of conducting business. Unfortunately, when it comes to leaders in our government, those at the top do not set the best examples. The government fails in this area with flying colors. Our government officials should be the people to stop all our country's problems, but they choose the divide and conquer technique, which prevents any positive advancement. The history of our time in this country shows how our government has led the people into disarray, confusion, and disorder. The government's laws show proof of failure.

We have all types of information about abuse, but we have no answers to explain or resolve it. Television commercials provide information that can help those who are mentally abused find help for their problems. When tragedies happens, like bombings or school shootings, people involved are provided with counseling and therapy. Most doctors only want to prescribe drugs to handle mental problems. They don't look at the whole picture of a person's life. A person's life revolves around work associations, family members, and other people they encounter on a daily basis. My doctors gave me some prescriptions and told me to go to work. I told them that the medicine compromised my concentration, and I would put people's safety in jeopardy if I went to work while taking them. The doctors told me I would have to deal with that problem, not them. I explained that I experienced dizziness and headaches, and yet they wanted me to take the drugs. Not only would I be irresponsible if I worked under the influence of the drugs, I would be breaking the law because it is illegal to work with heavy equipment while taking drugs that compromise mental and physical abilities. It is considered abuse by doctors when they ignore this, and it can lead to malpractice lawsuits and jail time.

People who have been advised to work while under the influence of prescription drugs have to find attorneys to handle their doctors' neglect. Attorneys often give their clients bullshit stories that the clients can't prove in court, and that is an example of legal neglect and abuse.

However, I have learned that, in Rhode Island at least, professional people don't go against each other in any way. Professional people (politicians, attorneys, judges, doctors, etc.) protect each other at all costs, including jeopardizing the lives of their clients and patient and the lives of their members as well. Once again, the government has the power to stop all this abusive activity, but the government allows the abusive problems to continue at all costs, and the cost quite often is money.

There are hundreds of types of mental disorders: anxiety disorders, dissociation disorders, mood disorders, trauma, and stressor-related disorders, neuro-developmental disorders, sleep-wake disorders, neuro-cognitive disorders, and substance-related and addictive disorders; the lists go on forever. Many symptoms and disorders overlap. Some people are born with mental disorders, and doctors do not entirely understand why that happens. Some people develop mental disorders after using street drugs and even some prescribed drugs. This can happen with young people as well as adults. Some people develop mental disorders after being in stressful situations like a war or a severe storm. And some people develop mental disorders after being treated improperly by other people in their families, workplaces, or community.

Professional people can treat their clients and patients improperly. They can play head games, and I know this from personal experience. The doctors couldn't figure out my problems, but I figured them out, and when I confronted the doctors, attorneys, and judges, they didn't like my answers. So they intentionally sabotaged my cases, which, in effect, also sabotaged my mind and body. Officials don't understand why someone whose life has been destroyed by a person or a government can need revenge and retaliation. That need can lead to tragedy for that person.

The problem with fibromyalgia is that not all doctors are willing to admit to the public or their patients that this illness exists and how dangerous it can be. I did a lot of research on reliable sources on the Internet and in books, but multiple doctors denied everything that I had learned. When I asked Attorney Moakley to use my research to support my case, he said that it hadn't come from a doctor. For my workers' compensation hearings, I had to submit all my medical reports and other documentation that I would be relying on. Moakley told me that my research could not be used as evidence in my case. When the COVID-19 pandemics hit the world, the officials from the CDC exerted influence over our government. Meanwhile, my attorney was telling me the information I got from the CDD website about fibromyalgia was not admissible as evidence.

Fibromyalgia causes pain and fatigue along with sleep, memory, and mood issues. It has been observed that stress can exacerbate related problems such as anxiety, depression, IBS, psychosis, panic attacks, and PTSD. The nervous system is compromised and patients can experience nerve damage. Secondary symptoms are different types of pains, confusion and fogginess, difficulty breathing, and headaches.

My personal tragedy came in the form of a boss who bullied his employees and threatened their jobs for no reason. Then it expanded as I spent years trying to get legal restitution for the damage he caused, both physical and mental. The worst part of all of this is that I tried to follow the law in my pursuit. Those in authority can break their own laws and get away with it, but a citizen can't do the slightest thing wrong without going to jail. So the odds are stacked against the citizens of America.

The symptoms of fibromyalgia can be devastating. I have done so much research on medical and legal information, and I believe that I know more than most professional people. I have only a high school education, and I have some trade college training. But I have the experience of having medical problems. The wonderful thing about technology is that so much information is available to everyone on the Internet. We should be able to use this information against the people who make and enforce the laws. The Internet is better than the law books that legal professionals refer to in their cases. The information from the Internet enables us to catch the lies of everyone involved with a case. It is the same with the medical information we can find online. With the information, we can challenge our doctors and their bullshit stories when they say they know what's wrong with us. The Internet provides the truth.

CHAPTER 34

STANDING ALONE WITH ATTORNEY KERRY DUNN AND JUDGE BETTY MACDUFF

I STOOD ALONE AFTER JUDGE MACDUFF ALLOWED ATTORNEY Moakley quit my case. Moakley had often left me standing alone to deal with all his mistakes rather than fighting for me as an attorney. Meanwhile, I was like David in the Bible story, and Judge Betty McDuff of the Workers' Compensation Office and Attorney Kerry Dunn from the town of Butland were my Goliaths: one against two. Incredibly, my chances of winning had diminished because I had no attorney, and McDuff was using the laws against me along with Dunn.

I had emailed Judge McDuff a month after Attorney Moakley quit and explained that I had to look for another attorney to take the case, but no one wanted it. My ability to obtain an attorney was complicated by the pandemic. The stress level within me was so high, and the pain was incredible throughout my body; I had been fighting for so long.

I was determined to push through this case in front of Judge Mac Duff and Attorney Dunn. I would try to prove the lies being used by Butland town representatives and Dunn. I would also show that Attorney Moakley had not done his job correctly. People in positions of power can often change the outcome of anything with their lies and corruption and support from their peers.

Judge MacDuff eventually answered my email and said that the hearing date was out of her control; she had nothing to do with selecting hearing dates. I thought it was odd that a judge would say those words; she and any other judge would say they would hear the case again in a week, a month, or six months. The lies all these people told were so incredible that they just blew my mind.

I had shown the truth and referenced the laws that applied to my case, but the people involved had just ignored or overruled me in order to avoid the situation. The problems were the same between Moakley and me. I got the runaround with no results.

Once again, I sent an email to Senior Judge Bill Child complaining about a hearing date. We had attended video conferences on time, but getting a hearing date was like pulling teeth from a stubborn animal. The sad part was that the animal was a human being who intentionally stopped the process of court procedures and due process of justice. I eventually heard from Senior Judge Child, but he just told me to stop bothering his office. Once again, he threatened me. He said he would call the cops and report that I was harassing judges. I did not get a proper response from him. Still, I responded to his email and told him that, if he categorized my emails to him and Judge MacDuff as harassment, he should just imagine a boss harassing a worker, discriminating against a worker, and bullying a worker. I told him I had no problems with the police getting involved with this matter. A police report might lead to an investigation to see if any criminal actions had taken place. Then maybe the truth would shine through, and my problems would be resolved with everybody involved with my two cases.

Unfortunately, nobody called the police for fear of incriminating themselves. I had got the runaround from everybody from the start.

Where do people go for justice and order when they have to deal with a corrupt legal system that includes government from the federal level all the way down to the town level? I think about following the laws, but they are controversial. People who are greedy and powerful cause a great deal of pain and hurt in countries all over the world. What will it take to straighten out our world and make it better? An act of God? Or worse, a third world war with nuclear weapons that could cause the extinction of all the men, women, and children on our earth? No matter what, we would be faced with chaos, and we would lose all hope because law and order would to be sustained by the government. We saw chaos in motion during the riots at the Capital on January 6, 2021. It is only the beginning of what is to come with our government and our future as a world. We have lost the foundations of government and society throughout the world because of greed and power. People of the world should put down their ignorance and work together for the betterment of everyone, equally and united together.

The rich, powerful, and greedy people are the poison of our world. This is reflected in the way my two cases progressed. Those in power were attorneys, doctors, and judges. These people can deliver justice or take justice away. I had been subjected to illegal treatment at my job. Legal and medical professionals with whom I was directly involved had refused to help me. Every agency I reached out to had ignored me.

So, how can a person report abuse carried out by our legal system? It's a system that doesn't want to hear its own problems. My friend, Attorney Norman Lake, told me that all I could do was write a book about my problems so that the world would know how badly I was treated by our legal and medical systems and other related systems. He also said that we have lost all respect for each other as people in our country, and the same probably has happened throughout the world too. I did not receive any respect as a citizen defending myself in front of attorneys and judges, but I still had to try. It is not easy for people who are not in the legal profession to obtain law books, and even those who do are not trained to understand the language or know how to research particular issues. Attorneys often refer to precedents set in old cases when presenting current cases, but the attorneys and judges use the references as laws when they are actually not; they are decisions based on law. Every case is unique. They may be similar but relying on case references may not always be a fair way of making a decision. The only time a reference may have absolute influence is if the law is changed to support it. It is written as a bill and approved by congress and the senate.

In our country, lawmakers and law enforcers use their interpretations of laws. If the system breaks down too far, people will revolt against our government. In our country, the riots at the Capital happened on January 6, 2021. Our government said that it is against the law to attack our government. But similar demonstrations have happened in our country for 245 years from the beginning of our government—1776—to the present time. The people have the right to question our government without any consequences.

Unfortunately, our government does enforce consequences. How could I challenge Judge MacDuff and Attorney Dunn? How could I prove that both of my cases had been negatively affected by fraud from the beginning?

Judge MacDuff and Attorney Dunn dragged my case out for many months in 2021. I occasionally spoke with my friend, Norman, and talk to him again about the case. He told me that I could not fix a broken system, and odds were against me. Once again, he advised me to settle and then write a book. Perhaps the book would solicit some help; at least I might be able to recover some of my losses from the sale of the book.

I emailed Judge MacDuff and told her that the town had offered me a settlement of $35,000. I told her I had originally agreed with Dunn on $50,000 at the mediation meeting, but the town of Butland had subsequently withdrawn that offer.

Judge MacDuff responded within an hour and said that she had learned nothing of any settlement discussions from either Moakley or Dunn. This was just another example of Moakley lying; he had not notified the judge about the settlement. Judge MacDuff said that she would look into this issue. In the email, she asked why I was trying to settle the case without going through the hearing. I told her that everybody involved with this case had acted improperly. I had lost everything—my personal life, my material possessions, and my health, which was worsening each day. My family members had suffered as well.

Judge MacDuff sent me another email and asked if I still wanted to settle by the end of the day. If I was serious about the settlement, the town of Butland and Dunn would agree only to $35,000, but that would be the end of the case. She said she would have a hearing date set if I agreed with the terms. I told her I agreed with the terms. A week later, I received a date for a hearing.

I told my mother I had agreed to settle, and the case was over. She agreed that was a good decision. She felt that my health might improve if my stress level lessened. I told her about Norman's suggestion to write a book, and she thought that was a good idea too.

Truthfully the settlement didn't feel right in my heart and my mind. I felt that the town and the attorneys had got away with beating me down. My mother said she thought that the town was paying for the problems they had caused through deceit, but I felt that the settlement was a one-time payment that wouldn't last for the rest of my life; what would I do when it ran out? My mother told me to take

Norman's advice, write the book, and see where it might take me. She said I might be shocked with the results; the book might inspire good things.

One week after my last email to Judge MacDuff, I attended a video hearing. Those present were Judge MacDuff, Attorney Kerry Dunn, and me. The judge reminded me that I would not be able to proceed with any complaints or legal actions once I received the settlement. She said that the town would not be responsible for any future problems that might arise as a result of anything pertaining to the case. She asked if I agreed to those terms and the amount of $35,000. I said I did. She asked Dunn if she understood the settlement terms. She said she did. The judge asked if either of us had any questions, and I told there was a lien against the case with the state of Rhode Island for state health insurance. The judge asked Dunn if she knew about this, and she said that the amount was $1,029. The judge asked if the town would cover the expense, and Dunn said it would. Then the judge signed the settlement. It was over.

When I asked how long it would be before I received a check, Dunn said that the legal time frame was two weeks after the signing, but she said she would need more. When the judge asked her how long, she said about four weeks. I said that I had waited seven long years for a check, and now they were asking for even more time! It seemed incredible to me. Judge MacDuff suggested that Dunn should get the check sooner, and she said she would try. I had one more question. Why had the town withdrawn the original settlement of $50,000? Judge MacDuff said that it was a different matter, and it hadn't been formally agreed upon in the previous proceedings. The judge then closed the hearing.

After four weeks, I had not received a check. I emailed judge Betty to let her know. I told her that the law gave the town two weeks, and she had granted Dunn four weeks, but still I had no check. I asked if I could receive penalties and interest. She said she would look into the issue; she would let me know within a month.

Another month later, on June 26, 2021, I received a check from the town of Butland that put an end to my workers' compensation case. Finally, I could turn my attention to writing my book. I didn't know anything about writing or publishing a book, and I didn't know if it would succeed once I finished it.

CHAPTER 35

THE CHALLENGES OF
WRITING A BOOK

I FOUND THAT THE PROCESS OF WRITING A BOOK WAS FILLED WITH challenges. I had so many unanswered questions. It's a good idea to have the necessary education and training when switching to a new career. I went to school for carpentry and construction, and I added to my skills and knowledge as I worked in my field over the years.

It had not been my idea to write this book; it had been the suggestion of a friend. I had never learned how to write anything professionally. When I was a young adult, I wrote a few love letters. When I was in business, I wrote estimates and contracts for customers. Once, I even wrote a diary for six months. Then I wrote a book in 2008, which was a precursor to this book.

I wrote this book to let the public know about the criminal actions that other people took during my seven-year legal battle. I know other people have experienced—or could experience— similar situations. White-collar crimes can devastate people and ruin lives. They can be perpetrated by anyone from any sector of society—private, business, and government. To me it is incredibly sad that nobody seems to care about each other anymore. To so many people and groups, life is all about power and greed. One man in a position of power ruined my life, and he was backed up by so many other professional people that I had no chance for justice.

Along with my inexperience in writing, my health posed a challenge as I began working on my book. I had to deal with pain, anxiety, and fatigue.

I started by gathering all my legal and medical records and all my correspondence. I had to make up new names for the characters in my book, and I had to keep a list to help me remember them! I kept a dictionary nearby to help me with spelling. My typing was not the best, and it slowed me down a bit, especially in the beginning. Even information from television news stories and commercials about medicine and abuse found its way into my story.

I worked from memory, referring the records as needed. A writer of fiction has the freedom to make up the entire story. A writer of nonfiction, however, must take care to present reality—the truth! I found that organizing and presenting the facts was difficult at first. I decided to write plainly and directly. I looked for the proper words that would best to describe what had really happened.

I had always wanted to change my career and do something other than carpentry and construction. I wanted a career in which I could use my mind rather than my muscle. Whenever I thought of writing, I thought of writing science fiction stories, not true-life stories, and especially my own life story—a tragedy.

Writing my story brought out so many emotions. I kept reliving my problems over and over again, experiencing rage, hurt, the pain of losing, feeling like a failure. It wasn't easy to reveal my feelings. I had never had to explain these feelings to anyone. No matter how hard we try to move forward in a positive direction, unfortunately, life goes through changes whether we like it or not. My life changed multiple times over seven long years with each up and down of my legal battle.

It was difficult to read through my medical and legal records because they contained so many lies. My original story and complaints had been changed so many times. Once the information was included in "official" documentation by professionals, nobody else would question it. In addition, I had done so much research about medical legal issues, and very little of this information matched my medical records or my legal experiences. It is unfortunate how far people had gone to distort the accurate information for the purpose of deceit. And I was sure I wasn't the only victim of such illegal practices.

As I worked and revisited my past, my fibromyalgia, PTSD, and anxiety symptoms would act up, and I would have to stop writing for a while. I was constantly reminded that the real criminals are the ones who have too much and use that leverage to compromise the lives of those who are less fortunate. Living my story was like being on a scary roller coaster, but writing my story was like experiencing my worst nightmare.

CHAPTER 36

NEWS MEDIA, TV COMMERCIALS, MEDICAL DOCUMENTS, AND LAWS

I HAVE WRITTEN MULTIPLE LETTERS TO LOCAL NEWSPAPERS AND NEWS stations asking them to investigate my story, but I never heard back from any of them. I have written multiple letters government offices asking them also to investigate, and I never heard back from any of them either.

The news people ask for tips about news stories, and the police use the media to request the public to provide information about crimes and criminals. But when a person asks the media for help in exposing criminal activity, they are nowhere to be found. And the same can be said about the police. It seems that these people are not willing to even look at instances of white-collar crime. But when citizens take things into their own hands, they find that their activities are against the laws of this country even though they are only defending their lives because the proper authorities have ignored their request for help. Then when the news media get the story, they cut it up in so many ways that it is not recognizable. The news media are interested only in ratings; they don't stand up for people by reporting accurate news. I believe that our government authorities tell the news media what to say and print; our news is censored. Big business also can influence news coverage when it is to their benefit.

In the film *Star Trek II: The Wrath of Khan* (written by Gene Rodenberry and Harve Bennet; story by Jack Sowards), the character Spock says "The needs of the many outweigh the needs of the few." So often this means that the needs of the wealthy and powerful outweigh the needs of the poor and helpless.

People are killed during tragedies such as the 9/11 attacks on the World Trade Center and the 2013 Boston Marathon bombing. White-collar crimes, on the other hand involve conspiracy, collusion, perjury, racketeering, slavery of all kinds, and so forth. Rhode Island's James "Whitey" Bulger was an organized crime boss until he was captured by the FBI. He was convicted of a number of crimes, some of which could be considered white-collar crimes. Richard Nixon's Watergate and Bill Clinton's White Water are examples of white-collar crimes in the government. Other white-collar crimes have gone undetected.

Bad things happen to people who come forward to report crimes committed by governments, leaders, secret societies, companies, and the rich and powerful.

The lower levels of society pay the price for the actions of the rich and powerful. They are used as examples, and they end up in prison. Do we have equal laws for everybody? Or are the laws different for the elite in society? We, the people, need to hold all people accountable and responsible for their criminal actions no matter the cost.

The professionals involved in my cases never had to answer for their crimes against me.

CHAPTER 37

THE HISTORY OF HUMANKIND

Humans have always been—and will always be—worse than any animal, and this has been going on since the beginning of time. Throughout our world, humans have been crude and obnoxious and warlike, existing for greed and power and control.

I believe that, no matter how "civilized" we as a race become, we will always be animals; we will destroy ourselves and many others. This happens on a personal level and escalates all the way up to international conflict. The goal is always wealth and power, and I don't see any resolution as we move into the future.

Unfortunately, we will never have peace and harmony; there will always be someone greedy who wants more power and wealth. The Bible tells us that God sent a flood to destroy our world and the people who had become wicked and sinful. God said that he would never interfere with the lives of humans again, but he did say that humans would kill themselves by fire and burn the world to a cinder. Then there would be a new start for the next generation. God also destroyed Sodom and Gomorrah because of the sexual corruption of the people

The Bible tells us that three people will try to control the world. Nostradamus, the French astrologer, predicted the end of our world as we know it now. Nostradamus also wrote about three men would destroy our world; two of them have passed by, but the third one is yet to come into our world. Could this be Vladimir Putin with his nuclear weapons? The predictions in the Bible and the writings of Nostradamus are becoming more and more evident in our world.

Today, even with our education and technology, people are no better than they were in ancient times. Weapons have become more deadly. World exploration inspired new levels of greed. Those in powerful position have always increased their power by exploiting those less fortunate than themselves.

During the Revolutionary War (1775 to 1783), those who would become Americans fought the English king, who wanted more financial support from the colonists in America. Our freedom was declared in 1776, and the people fought for a better country for the people, but they only carried their problems with them from the Old World to the New World.

Later, when Americans started to expand across the land, they fought multiple wars with Indian nations, the first war with the British and the second war with the Indian nations, the original owners of this land. White people forced their religion on the indigenous people and forced them to give up their culture because they considered them an inferior race. Then white people enslaved black people. The Civil War—the North against the South—was fought for the freedom of enslaved people. In our history, leaders have started wars, and they have forced poor people to fight. The leaders stay alive and earn large profits and positions of power. Many on the battlefield are wounded or die. Those who survive do not benefit. This applies to all the wars ever fought on every continent of our world.

Our Earth provides everything we need to sustain life, but our governments are expanding into space to find resources and even other life-sustaining planets to conquer. I don't believe that alien races will tolerate the problems of humanity. I believe that aliens are far ahead of us in knowledge and technology. They are more powerful than we are. And I like to think that they are socially more advanced as well.

The possibility of an alien invasion of earth is strong, especially if we continue our plans to plunder other planets without consequences. Aliens are aware of the destruction we do to our planet and each other.

Our government is socializing with aliens, and then the feed us lies that we are the only race in the universe. Anyone with a brain knows that there is something more in our universe than us. A race of animals, reptiles, and people just didn't pop up from the dirt or float through space. We all came from somewhere in the universe; the question is where? Remember, we all have only one chance to get things right between ourselves and any other race in our universe.

CHAPTER 38

FINAL THOUGHTS EIGHT
YEARS LATER

After I finished writing my book, I faced the challenge of publishing it. I was not familiar with the process.

The health conditions I suffered with during my seven years of legal battles have worsened over the years, and new conditions have developed. I don't think my doctors followed their Hippocratic oath or practiced proper protocol. And they didn't follow the law. Many people I've shared my story with have told me that I should never have had to suffer such devastating mental and physical issues. Many agreed with me that medical and legal professionals and the many people I wrote to asking for help had taken advantage of my situation. I never got the help and support I needed from those who had the power to give it to me. They looked the other way when I desperately needed them. I felt like a solitary man up against a bunch of bullies.

When politicians campaign for office, they say what the voters want to hear. Most people don't realize—or don't want to know—that they are lying and avoiding the issues. They care about their constituents or their problems. Once they are in office, everything they said in those fine speeches flies out the window while they sign up for kickbacks and plan their re-election strategies. The COVID-19 pandemic is a good example. The government shut down the world, but the rich and powerful had enough money so their lives didn't change much. Those with fewer monetary resources struggled to survive, both financially and emotionally.

So many people all across the world are struggling somehow, but no one needs the problems that arise when people make things harder than they should be. For years I've heard people say that this is the only government and legal system we have, and we need laws so we can maintain order among the people. It is time to make changes in our government, and there cannot be any questions from the politicians. Remember, we elect, support, and pay our government officials through our taxes. Is the present chaotic state of our government the thanks we get from our government? The people of the United States should take back this from those who are abusing their power, and they should hold the politicians and other officials responsible for their actions.

My journey has come to an end—for now. I am so grateful for my family members, my girlfriend, and the people who showed me kindness along the way even though they were unable to help me.

Printed in the United States
by Baker & Taylor Publisher Services